Intro to Business

SECOND EDITION

Robert A. Ristau

Australia • Brazil • Japan • Korea • Mexico • Singapore • Spain • United Kingdom • United States

SOUTH-WESTERN
CENGAGE Learning·

21st Century Business
Intro to Business, 2nd Edition
Robert A. Ristau

Editorial Director: Jack W. Calhoun

Vice President/Editor-in-Chief: Karen Schmohe

Executive Editor: Eve Lewis

Senior Developmental Editor: Penny Shank

Editorial Assistant: Anne Kelly

Marketing Manager: Diane Morgan

Technology Project Manager: Lysa Kosins

Content Project Management: Pre-Press PMG

Senior Manufacturing Buyer: Kevin Kluck

Production Service: Pre-Press PMG

Senior Art Director: Tippy McIntosh

Internal Design: Pre-Press PMG

Cover Designer: Lou Ann Thesing

Cover Image: Getty Images, iStock

Permission Acquisitions Manager/Text:
   Mardell Glinkski-Schultz

Permission Acquisitions Manager/Photo:
   Deanna Ettinger

For product information and technology assistance, contact us at
Cengage Learning Customer & Sales Support, 1-800-354-9706
For permission to use material from this text or product,
submit all requests online at **www.cengage.com/permissions**
Further permissions questions can be emailed to
permissionrequest@cengage.com

Library of Congress Control Number: 2009942195

Student Edition ISBN 13: 978-0-538-74066-1

Student Edition ISBN 10: 0-538-74066-3

South-Western Cengage Learning
5191 Natorp Boulevard
Mason, OH 45040
USA

Cengage Learning products are represented in Canada by Nelson Education, Ltd.

For your course and learning solutions, visit **cengage.com/school**

Printed in China
2 3 4 5 6 7 13 12

The *21st Century Business Series* is an innovative instructional program providing instructors with the greatest flexibility to deliver business content using a modular format. Instructors can create their own business courses by combining several **Learner Guides** in the *Series* to form one-semester or two-semester courses. The individual **Learner Guides** can also be used as enhancements to more traditional business courses or to tailor new courses to meet emerging needs.

The design and content of each **Learner Guide** in the *21st Century Business Series* are engaging yet easy for students to use. The content focuses on providing opportunities for applying 21st Century business skills while enabling innovative learning methods that integrate the use of supportive technology and creative problem-solving approaches in today's business world.

The *Intro to Business* **Learner Guide** covers today's most relevant business topics such as how business has been affected by the global economic crisis and recovery as well as global environmental issues. The roles of marketing and human resources management are also incorporated into this **Learner Guide.**

ORGANIZED FOR SUCCESS

Each chapter opens with a **Project** that incorporates information from each lesson within the chapter. These **Projects** pull all of the information from the chapter together so students get a hands-on experience applying what they learned, making for a great group activity.

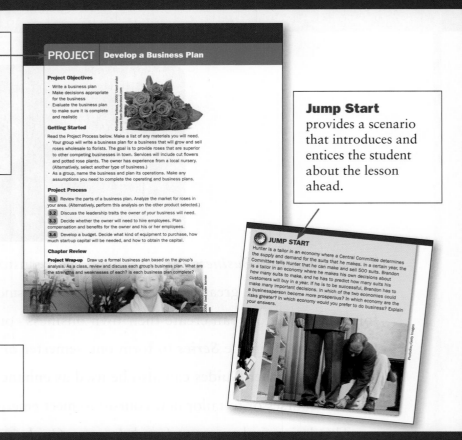

PROJECT Develop a Business Plan

Project Objectives
· Write a business plan
· Make decisions appropriate for the business
· Evaluate the business plan to make sure it is complete and realistic

Getting Started
Read the Project Process below. Make a list of any materials you will need.
· Your group will write a business plan for a business that will grow and sell roses wholesale to florists. The goal is to provide roses that are superior to other competing businesses in town. Services will include cut flowers and potted rose plants. The owner has experience from a local nursery. (Alternatively, select another type of business.)
· As a group, name the business and plan its operations. Make any assumptions you need to complete the operating and business plans.

Project Process
3.1 Review the parts of a business plan. Analyze the market for roses in your area. (Alternatively, perform this analysis on the other product selected.)
3.2 Discuss the leadership traits the owner of your business will need.
3.3 Decide whether the owner will need to hire employees. Plan compensation and benefits for the owner and his or her employees.
3.4 Develop a budget. Decide what kind of equipment to purchase, how much start-up capital will be needed, and how to obtain the capital.

Chapter Review
Project Wrap-up Draw up a formal business plan based on the group's analysis. As a class, review and discuss each group's business plan. What are the strengths and weaknesses of each? Is each business plan complete?

Jump Start provides a scenario that introduces and entices the student about the lesson ahead.

Net Bookmark gives chapter-related activities for students to complete using information found on the Internet.

JUMP START

Hunter is a tailor in an economy where a Central Committee determines the supply and demand for the suits that he makes. In a certain year, the Committee tells Hunter that he can make and sell 500 suits. Brandon is a tailor in an economy where he makes his own decisions about how many suits to make, and he has to predict how many suits his customers will buy in a year. If he is to be successful, Brandon has to make many important decisions. In which of the two economies could a businessperson become more prosperous? In which economy are the risks greater? In which economy would you prefer to do business? Explain your answers.

REAL-WORLD FOCUS

Cross-Cultural Relationships highlights the importance of understanding and respecting everyone's point of view and thinking about the perspectives of others.

Throughout the book, you will find **Business Math Connection**. This feature highlights how basic math concepts are an important part of the business world.

Tech Literacy

TECHNOLOGY TOOLS
When it comes to creating a business plan, help is available on the Internet. A quick search using the keywords "business plan template" or "business plan sample," finds numerous matches. A template allows you to plug in specific information to create a professional-looking business plan.

THINK CRITICALLY
What do you see as some advantages and disadvantages of using a business plan template?

Tech Literacy highlights how evolving technology plays a huge role in how business is conducted.

Business Math Connection

Calculate the net profit or loss for the month for Galaxy Comic Books where cash sales were $3,560, charge sales were $1,240, and other revenue was $165. Salaries were $2,450, advertising was $200, rent was $550, and supplies were $120.

SOLUTION
The formula for calculating net profit or loss is

Revenue − Expenses = Profit (or Loss)

$(3,560 + 1,240 + 165) − (2,450 + 200 + 550 + 120) = $ Profit (or Loss)

$4,965 − 3,320 = 1,645$

The net profit was $1,645.

TEAMWORK

Work in teams to make a list of property that various team members own. Note the type of property owned. What is the most common type? Discuss the importance of being able to own property. What rights and responsibilities go along with property ownership?

Teamwork provides an activity that requires the students to work together as a team.

HANDS-ON LEARNING

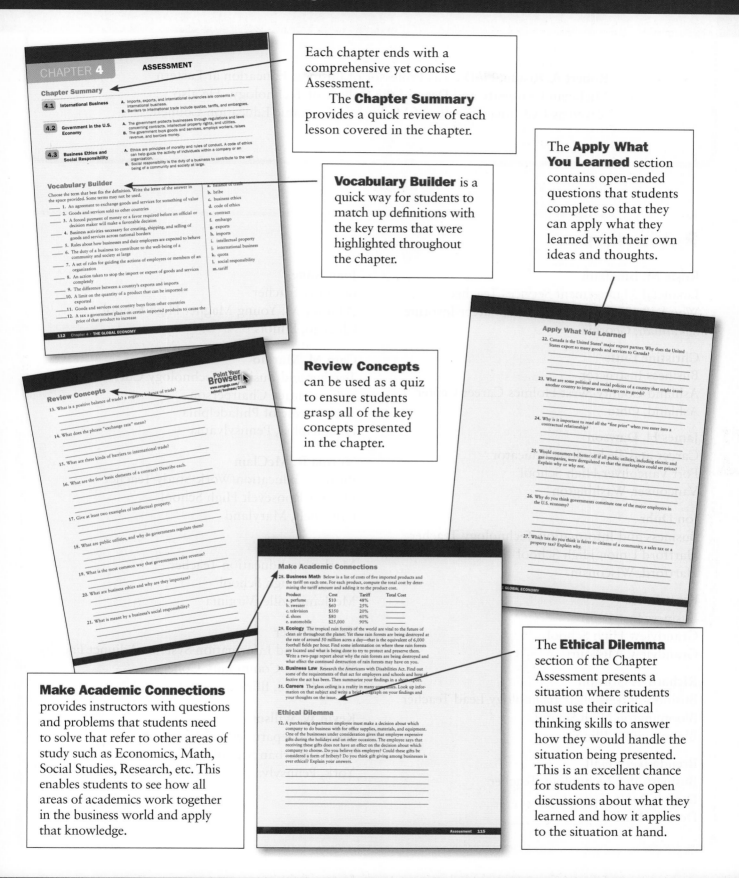

Each chapter ends with a comprehensive yet concise Assessment.

The **Chapter Summary** provides a quick review of each lesson covered in the chapter.

Vocabulary Builder is a quick way for students to match up definitions with the key terms that were highlighted throughout the chapter.

The **Apply What You Learned** section contains open-ended questions that students complete so that they can apply what they learned with their own ideas and thoughts.

Review Concepts can be used as a quiz to ensure students grasp all of the key concepts presented in the chapter.

Make Academic Connections provides instructors with questions and problems that students need to solve that refer to other areas of study such as Economics, Math, Social Studies, Research, etc. This enables students to see how all areas of academics work together in the business world and apply that knowledge.

The **Ethical Dilemma** section of the Chapter Assessment presents a situation where students must use their critical thinking skills to answer how they would handle the situation being presented. This is an excellent chance for students to have open discussions about what they learned and how it applies to the situation at hand.

ABOUT THE AUTHOR

Robert A. Ristau, Ph.D., was Professor of Business Education at Eastern Michigan University and Dean of the College of Technology. He also served as Executive Director of Michigan's Economic Education Council.

Reviewers

Rosie M. Bingham
Financial Management Services Teacher
Woodville-Tompkins Technical Career Institute
Savannah, Georgia

Christine Butts
Business Instructor
Ashland County-West Holmes Career Center
Ashland, Ohio

James H. Dawson
Career and Technology Educator
Fort Vancouver High School
Vancouver, Washington

Jon Duhr
Business and Information Technology Teacher
Hartford Union High School
Hartford, Wisconsin

Ernst Fields
Business Instructor
Grandview High School
Grandview, Missouri

Richard T. Gordon
Business and Applied Technology Lead Teacher
Bloomington High School
Bloomington, Illinois

Brenda Ivery Hall
Business and Technology Teacher
Detroit Public Schools
Detroit, Michigan

Joan Kane
Business Teacher
Whitney M. Young Magnet High School
Chicago, Illinois

Cara M. Marino
Teacher and Business Technology Curriculum
    Committee Chairperson
Archdiocese of Philadelphia
Philadelphia, Pennsylvania

Norma R. McClain
Business Education/Work-Study Teacher
Eleanor Roosevelt High School
Greenbelt, Maryland

Richard Totten
Marketing Education Teacher
Hanover High School
Mechanicsville, Virginia

Tricia Troyer
Business and Information Systems Adjunct Faculty
Waubonsee Community College
Sugar Grove, Illinois

Kevin W. Willson
Business Department Chairperson
York Suburban School District
York, Pennsylvania

CONTENTS

The Economic Environment

Careers in Business

Government & Public Administration

UNITED STATES POSTAL SERVICE

The United States Postal Service (USPS) provides important services for our economy. It distributes letters and packages throughout our nation and the world and transmits money through postal money orders.

In a recent year, the Postal Service employed more than 700,000 workers. Job openings are posted on USPS.com.

A high-visibility Postal Service job is the window service clerk. Tasks include greeting customers, selling stamps, weighing mail for correct postage, selling money orders, handling passports, checking packages for mailing, and selling post office merchandise.

The job requirements include a high school diploma or GED. Applicants must pass a written test and are then placed on a "roster" and ranked based on their test score. If selected for an opening, they are interviewed. Consideration is given to factors relevant to this job, such as the applicant's work record, administrative skills, and ability to work with people.

Think Critically

1. Would you consider a career in the U.S. Postal Service? Why or why not?
2. What do you find interesting about the window service clerk's job?

PROJECT | Supply and Demand

Project Objectives

- Describe the concepts of supply and demand in your own words
- Discuss how supply and demand affect prices

©Alhovik, 2009/ Used under license from Shutterstock.com

Getting Started

Read the Project Process below.
Make a list of any materials you will need.

- Look at all the information you will gather for this project and decide how to put it into a format that is easy to understand.
- Make a list of three products purchased by you or your family whose prices tend to change.
- Next to each item on your list, write the current price for a certain quantity. For example, gasoline might be selling at $3.19 per gallon.

Project Process

1.1 List major producers of your listed items. What impact might this competition have on the price of these items?

1.2 Decide whether the items listed are needs or wants. In what step of the economic decision-making process do you consider price? Why?

1.3 Would you continue to buy these items if the nation were in a recession? in a depression? Why?

1.4 Predict what would happen to the price of your listed items if the quantity available doubled. Predict what would happen to the price if the supply were cut in half. Would you buy more or less in each case? Why?

Chapter Review

Project Wrap-up Create a visual presentation of the results of your research. Include the current price of your listed items. If any prices have changed, present a theory of why the change may have occurred.

©Mikhail Olykainen, 2009/ Used under license from Shutterstock.com

GOALS

Compare three types of economies

Describe and explain the characteristics of a market economy

KEY TERMS

scarcity, p. 4

market economy, p. 5

capitalism, p. 6

profit, p. 7

competition, p. 8

 JUMP START

Hunter is a tailor in an economy where a Central Committee determines the supply and demand for the suits that he makes. In a certain year, the Committee tells Hunter that he can make and sell 500 suits. Brandon is a tailor in an economy where he makes his own decisions about how many suits to make, and he has to predict how many suits his customers will buy in a year. If he is to be successful, Brandon has to make many important decisions. In which of the two economies could a businessperson become more prosperous? In which economy are the risks greater? In which economy would you prefer to do business? Explain your answers.

Photodisc/Getty Images

Economic Systems

Our businesses operate in a global marketplace and deal with a variety of economic systems that influence each other. Countries take different approaches in how their economies operate, but each must provide answers to the same basic economic questions.

Economic Problem

All types of economic systems face similar problems. The most basic economic problem is referred to as scarcity. **Scarcity** is the conflict between unlimited wants and limited resources. In order to decide how to use its scarce resources, a country must answer three key economic questions. The answers to these questions depend in large part on the society's economic system.

1. *What to produce?* Should resources be used to provide consumer goods, industrial goods, or military goods?

2. *How should things be produced?* What kinds of industries and equipment should be used?

3. *For whom should they be produced?* Which of its citizens should benefit most from what is produced?

Types of Economic Systems

An economic system refers to the way in which a society provides things that are desired by its citizens. Economic systems can be classified into traditional, command, or market economies. Today, the market economy is the most common; however, most economies tend to be mixed and have elements of both traditional and command economies. Few are purely just one kind or the other.

Traditional Economy In a traditional economy, things are done according to tradition and progress is very slow. This type of economy may be found in developing or third-world countries. Goods are produced with techniques and processes handed down from generation to generation. Goods typically are produced by hand with simple tools. Change and growth occur slowly, and people generally are poor in material goods.

Command Economy
In a command economy, the government owns the businesses and controls the economy. Officials, usually through central committees, make decisions on what and how goods are produced and how they will be shared. They decide how much resources will be spent on the military and how much will be spent on consumer goods. Government officials plan all phases of the economy and command that the plans be carried out. Citizens have little say on how the three key economic questions are answered, and people have limited freedoms.

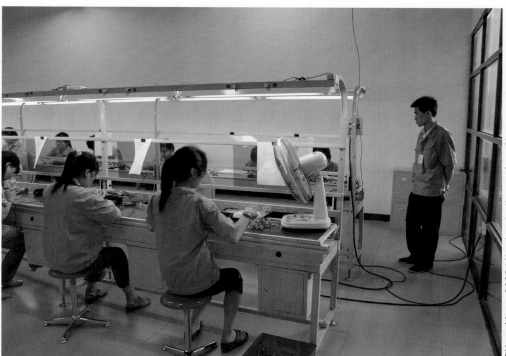

©Hugo Maes, 2009/ Used under license from Shutterstock.com

Who decides what products to make in a command economy?

Market Economy In a **market economy**, businesses and individuals are free to make their own decisions as they buy and sell in the marketplace.

NETBookmark

A "mixed economy" is an economic system that combines elements of market and command economies. Access www.cengage.com/school/business/21biz and click on the link for Chapter 1. Read the article, and then name at least three examples of government regulation in a mixed economy. What is a disadvantage of a mixed economy? Do you agree with the article that the U.S. economy is a mixed economy? Explain.

www.cengage.com/school/business/21biz

Market economies generally are found in countries that have a democratic form of government. Market economies, such as the U.S. economy, often are said to be practicing capitalism or free enterprise. **Capitalism** means that economic resources are privately owned by individuals rather than by the government. Individual owners of businesses are free to decide what they will produce, which is the basis for the term *free enterprise*. In a market economy, decisions about production and distribution are largely made by voluntary exchange in the *marketplace* where sellers and buyers do business.

CheckPOINT

What is the major difference between a command economy and a market economy? Is that difference important to you? Why or why not?

_____

_____

Characteristics of Market Economies

There are a number of important characteristics that help us identify a market economy. Four of these are private enterprise, private property, profit, and competition.

Private Enterprise

Businesses supply you with products and services in exchange for a payment of some kind. An individual's right to own a business, select a market to enter, and produce with limited government direction is called *private enterprise*. The private enterprise economy is based on freedom of choice. As the owner of a business in private enterprise, you are free to succeed or fail. Private enterprise gives you the right to start any business you wish and operate it as you want as long as you obey the laws that regulate the business. Some regulations are necessary even in a market economy to protect people from harm. For instance, if your company deals with hazardous waste materials, you must obey laws about how to dispose of those materials.

Cross-Cultural Relationships

ECONOMIES AROUND THE WORLD

The economic success of market economies has caused many countries to reexamine their economic systems. Many command economies have not prospered in comparison to market economies. Command economies are not designed to meet the wants and needs of the individual. In most command economies, workers with different skills and responsibilities basically receive the same wages. There is little incentive for people to work hard and increase production.

The weaknesses of command economies have caused many nations throughout the world to change to a market economy. A notable example is the former Soviet Union. For many years, the people there were forced to do without goods such as home appliances and adequate housing. Other countries once part of the Soviet Bloc—including Poland, Hungary, and the Czech Republic—have made great strides toward establishing new market economies. These economies now benefit from voluntary exchange in the marketplace.

Think Critically

What are some of the benefits to the citizens of a country that converts its economic system from a command economy to a market system?

TEAMWORK

Work in teams to make a list of property that various team members own. Note the type of property owned. What is the most common type? Discuss the importance of being able to own property. What rights and responsibilities go along with property ownership?

Private Property

Your right to *private property* means that you can own, use, and dispose of things of value. If you listen to music on a laptop that you own, you are enjoying the right of private property. You can own any item and do what you want with it as long as you do not violate a law that has been enacted to protect others' rights. You also can own, use, and sell whatever you create. Businesses also have the right to own property. This property can include land, buildings, tools, and the goods the business produces.

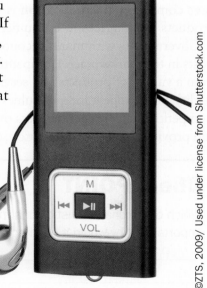

©ZTS, 2009/ Used under license from Shutterstock.com

What does the right to private property mean to you?

Profit

In economies like ours, an important characteristic is your right to earn a profit. **Profit** is

Why is competition important in the marketplace?

the amount of money left over when subtracting the expenses of operating a business from its income—it is a reward for taking risks. Profit is important to business owners because it pays them for the time and money they have invested in their businesses. The desire to work hard, to be creative, and to satisfy customers in order to earn a profit is called the *profit motive*. The profit motive has helped market economies outperform the other types of economies.

Competition

Earning a profit in a market economy is not easy. A good business will always have competition. **Competition** is the rivalry among businesses to sell their products and services to consumers.

Governments with market economies enact laws to help assure that competition exists in the marketplace. Competition gives consumers the opportunity to choose from a variety of products and services. These choices are made by comparing the quality, price, appearance, usefulness, and general appeal of products and services. Competition encourages business owners to improve their products and services and provide a superior product or service at a competitive price.

CheckPOINT

Which of the characteristics of a market economy do you believe is the most important? Why would it be important to you as a business owner? as a citizen?

_____

_____

_____

Think Critically

1. Why have market economies been adopted in many countries throughout the world that formerly had command economies?

_____

_____

_____

2. If you were a citizen in a country that converted from a traditional economy to a market economy, what are some of the changes that you would find in your life compared to life under the former system?

_____

_____

_____

3. What do you think are the positive and negative aspects of the profit motive in a market economy?

_____

_____

_____

4. What are some things that a government can do to help assure that there is fair competition in the marketplace?

_____

_____

_____

Make Academic Connections

5. **Communication** A student from a country with a command economy has come to your school. Write a letter to the student explaining how a market economy differs from a command economy.

6. **Research** China basically has a command economy. Using the Internet and other sources, find out what China is doing now to give more freedom to businesses, allowing them to conduct business in a free market economy. Write a brief report on your findings.

7. **Geography** Make a list of countries that, in the past several years, have converted their economic systems to a market system. Then obtain a world map and locate these countries. Color those countries that historically have had a market economy in one color, and color the countries that have come to the market economy system later in another color.

JUMP START

Brianna and Brittney love to bake cookies, and they have developed their own special recipe. They also have learned how to make cookies in a variety of special shapes and sizes. Their friends rave about their cookies, so they decided to start their own business: Busy B's Bakery. When they started planning their business, they were surprised by the many decisions they had to make: where to locate, what equipment to buy, how to get out the word about their new cookies, to name a few. They gathered information and made decisions as a team. They could not afford all the new equipment they wanted, so they bought used equipment that met their needs. Have there been times when you settled for something that satisfied your needs rather than your wants?

Photodisc/Getty Images

Providing Needs and Wants

The needs and wants of a society are met through the production of goods and services. This production requires the use of economic resources. Those who participate in the economy must go through an economic decision making process to help choose among the many alternatives available to meet their needs and wants.

Needs and Wants

Needs are things required in order to live. Food, water, clothing, and housing are basic things that people need. **Wants** are things that are not necessary for survival, but add comfort and pleasure to your life. You may want a Blu-ray player, a smart phone, or a new athletic jacket—but you can get along without them. It is important for you to be able to distinguish between your needs and your wants.

Goods and Services

Most needs and wants are satisfied with goods and services. **Goods** are things you can see and touch. Cell phones, electronic book readers, school rings, iPods, and sports equipment are examples of goods. In the marketplace, goods are generally referred to as *products*.

Not all needs and wants can be satisfied with goods. **Services** are activities that are consumed at the same time they are produced. The hairstylist who cuts your hair or the serviceperson who repairs your computer performs services you purchase. When you deposit a token to get a car wash, you are buying a service.

Economic Resources

Goods cannot be produced by magic or created out of nothing. Services must be produced through the efforts of people or equipment. The means through which goods and services are produced are called **economic resources** or *factors of production*. There are three kinds of economic resources: natural, human, and capital. Each of these is necessary to produce goods and services that meet needs and wants.

Natural Resources Raw materials supplied by nature are called *natural resources*. These come from the earth, water, or the air. Iron ore and oil are mined or pumped from the earth to use in making many goods. Vegetables grown in the soil and fish taken from the waters satisfy our need for food. Hospitals use oxygen extracted from the air to help aid patients. The goods we use today begin with at least one natural resource.

Human Resources Important as they are, natural resources cannot satisfy needs and wants by themselves. It takes people to turn them into goods and services and make them available. *Human resources* are the people who work to produce goods and services. *Labor* is another term used in referring to human resources. Human resources include people who operate farms and factories, manage banks, design machines, process food, forecast the weather, and police the streets.

Capital Resources The tools, equipment, supplies, and buildings that are used to supply goods and services are called *capital resources*. Factories, offices, road building equipment, computers, cash registers, smart phones, and display cases are examples of capital resources. Cars and trucks used to deliver newspapers are capital equipment. So are grills used to prepare hamburgers and other foods.

Money is a type of capital resource and is sometimes referred to as *capital*. Capital is used to start, operate, or expand a business. Obtaining sufficient

DID YOU KNOW ?

The economic resource of power prior to the time of our Industrial Revolution was 95% "muscle power;" now it is less than 1%. Power today is enhanced through the use of many kinds of mechanical equipment and computer technology.

capital is one of the first major steps in starting a business. A business firm may try to raise $1 million to expand its operation, or an individual may need $15,000 to start a small business. Sufficient capital is important to success in business.

All three economic resources—natural, human, and capital—are needed to produce goods and services to satisfy needs and wants. These resources are not unlimited. Natural resources, if not properly managed, can be used up. Capital may be difficult to raise, and needed equipment may be unavailable. Qualified workers may be unavailable or in short supply. These limitations are important in an economy and can cause individuals, businesses, and countries to compete for access and ownership of economic resources.

Photodisc/Getty Images

What economic resources are represented in this photo?

Economic Decision Making

Because you cannot have everything you need and want, you must make choices that enable you to have the things that you want most and can afford. For instance, say you have $35 to spend. If you spend that money going to a movie and then having a pizza, you may not have enough money to go to a sporting event you also want to attend. If you buy a new shirt that you like, you may not be able to buy a new video game that a friend recommended. These are examples of economic decisions that you could make and the alternatives that could be affected.

Economic decision making is the process of deciding among several alternative wants to determine the one most desired. There is a process involved, and once you learn it, decision making becomes easier and the decisions are better. Whether the decision is major or minor, the decision-making model that follows will help you to make wise economic decisions.

CheckPOINT

Which of the three economic resources do you feel is the most important? Explain why.

_____

_____

Tech Literacy

COMPUTERS IN BUSINESS

One of the most important capital resources for American businesses is computers and related technology products. New technology constantly makes older technology obsolete, so businesses must keep their computer-dependent employees equipped with efficient computers that work with the latest technology.

The popularity of e-commerce, the buying and selling over the Internet, has increased the demand for website design, maintenance, and support. Businesses also use the Web to create business-to-business relationships that support the purchase and sale of products and services. Computers provide important links between businesses.

THINK CRITICALLY

Explain why computers and related technology are increasingly important to the U.S. economy.

Decision-Making Process

The process of decision making is illustrated in the following six-step decision-making model used by many businesses and individuals. It involves defining the problem, identifying choices, exploring choices, making a choice, acting on the choice, and reviewing the decision after acting on it.

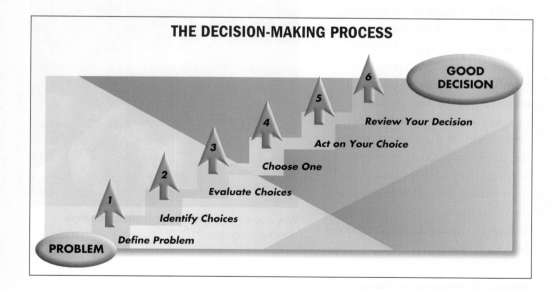

THE DECISION-MAKING PROCESS

GOOD DECISION

6 — Review Your Decision

5 — Act on Your Choice

4 — Choose One

3 — Evaluate Choices

2 — Identify Choices

1 — Define Problem

PROBLEM

Step 1 Define the Problem

This is the most important step. If you don't clearly define what you want to achieve, you may end up starting over. Suppose you say that your problem is that you have to decide what you will do this weekend. This seems specific enough, but questions remain. How much money do you have to spend? What activities are available this weekend?

A more clearly defined problem would be whether to go to a movie or to a concert with friends. A clear definition of the problem helps you focus your attention.

Step 2 Identify the Choices

Before you can make a choice, you must research what choices are available to you. For the example in step one, you would want to find out what movies of interest are offered and what concerts are scheduled for the weekend. You would want to ask your friends if they want to go to a movie or a concert, and if so, which they would prefer. You would also consider the costs associated with each choice.

Step 3 Evaluate Each Choice

At this point, you have quite a bit of information. You would then evaluate the advantages and disadvantages of each choice. Suppose some of your friends want to go to a movie that was just released. If you go to an afternoon matinee, it would cost less than if you go in the evening. What you buy for snacks while in the theater also adds to the cost. Concerts usually cost more than a movie, but the live performance may mean something very special to you.

You can see that there are a number of factors to consider, including price and personal satisfaction, when making an evaluation of the choices in the decision-making process. Writing down your choices and then listing the advantages and disadvantages of each choice is a technique many decision-makers find to be helpful.

Why should you evaluate your choices before making a decision?

©Zibedik, 2009/ Used under license from Shutterstock.com

Step 4 Choose One

This is the step in which you make a choice based on all of the information you have gathered. You now have a good idea of what options you may choose from, and you know how much each item costs. You know that choosing either the concert or the movie would keep you within your budget.

Suppose most of your friends want to go to the concert. You might plan to see the new movie next weekend. Your choice is to go to the concert, and you hope to see the new movie when it is shown again at a later date.

Step 5 Act on Your Choice

In this step, you take action and follow up on your choice. This may require a number of tasks and some planning. For example, you would have to determine how many friends want to go to the concert. Someone would have to order and possibly pick up the tickets. More than one driver may be needed to get all of you to the concert. You may also have to decide when and where you would meet to get to the concert. Acting on your choice to go to the concert with your friends requires some more planning.

Once you have made a decision, what should you do next?

Step 6 Review Your Decision

Whenever you make a decision, it is important to review your decision. Sometimes you will be happy with your decision and sometimes you won't. Using the decision-making process is no guarantee that every decision you make will make you happy. A decision to go to an outdoor concert might be spoiled when an unexpected rainstorm develops and the concert is cancelled at the last minute.

Using the decision-making process cannot prevent unexpected events. The next time the group considers going to an outdoor concert they might consider an alternative and have a backup plan. Reviewing past decisions can help you better understand how to make a good decision in the future.

TEAMWORK

As a team, come up with a decision-making problem that a typical student might face. Use the first four steps in the decision-making process to come to a decision. Then, present your team's problem and decision to the class, stating which of the four steps was the most difficult.

CheckPOINT

Which of the six steps in the decision-making process do you think is the most important? Give reasons for your answer.

_____

_____

Think Critically

1. Why are there so many wants in our society? Why aren't people content with just meeting their needs?

   _____

   _____

   _____

2. You are, or will be, among the most important economic resources—human resources, a worker in the U.S. economy. What are some of the things that you and others should do to help assure that U.S. human resources are the best that they can be?

   _____

   _____

   _____

3. Many people make careless and uninformed decisions, refusing to take the time they need to make good decisions. What do you think are some reasons why people do this?

   _____

   _____

   _____

4. There is no such thing as a perfect decision, only a very good decision based on information available at the time of the decision. What kind of attitude is best to have toward a decision once it is made?

   _____

   _____

   _____

Make Academic Connections

5. **Ecology** Search articles in magazines or newspapers or on the Internet for information relating to the use of our natural resources. List some of the abuses and some of the activities that are being done to protect and conserve our natural resources.

6. **Marketing** Go through a newspaper or magazine and read the advertisements. What do these advertisements emphasize? How do they affect your wants? Write one page describing your thoughts about wants and needs in relation to commercial advertising.

JUMP START

The Busy B's Bakery got off to a good start. Several stores began selling Busy B cookies, and customers loved them. Orders increased and additional workers had to be hired. But then something unexpected happened: the economy slowed down. Many people lost their jobs, and because of that, the demand for products, such as Busy B cookies, decreased. For a while, Brianna and Brittney could hardly meet expenses. They had to lay off their workers. By cutting other business costs, they managed to stay in business until the economy recovered and the demand for their cookies increased. Although their business was good once again, should they look ahead and make plans for another downturn in the economy?

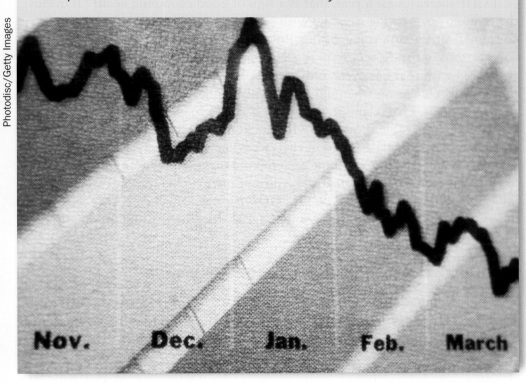

Nov.   Dec.   Jan.   Feb.   March

Economic Measurements

One of the goals of an economy is to be healthy—to have a steady growth in the production of goods and services. The health of a nation's economy is measured in several ways. High employment and a low rate of business failures are two indicators of a healthy economy.

An important part of life is measuring performance. The grade you receive is a measurement of your performance in class. A point guard in basketball who averages 21 points and 6 assists per game is a valuable player. An increase in your savings account is a measurement of good money management.

Three measurements used in looking at the health of an economy are gross domestic product, labor productivity, and inflation and deflation.

Gross Domestic Product

Gross domestic product (GDP) is the total dollar value of all goods and services produced in an economy in one year. It is a basic measurement of how an economy is doing. Information is collected from producers, and data is gathered on the value of what is being produced, called *output*. GDP includes four major categories.

1. Consumer spending for food, clothing, and housing
2. Business spending for buildings, equipment, and supplies
3. Government spending to pay employees and to buy supplies and other goods and services
4. The exports of a country less the imports of the country

If GDP increases each year, that is a sign of good economic health. It means the economy is growing steadily. With GDP growing, there are more jobs and consumer satisfaction is increasing. Prices increase over the years. To make comparisons accurate, a *base year* is established. Prices in any year are then compared with that base year. Otherwise, price increases can make it appear that GDP is increasing when output actually is not increasing. When the effect of price increases is taken out, this result is called *constant dollar* or *real GDP*.

The following table shows GDP for the fictitious nation of Technoland which produces Techlatts, used in energy-saving ecoblatts. Technoland's GDP is shown in current and constant prices. Note the differences in the figures for GDP in each of those categories. Current price GDP takes into account inflation and has higher GDP figures. *GDP per capita*, which is another way to measure economic growth, is the total GDP divided by the total population.

GDP COMPARISONS OF TECHNOLAND					
Year	Number of Techlatts Produced	Current Price per Techlatt	GDP at Current Prices	Prices Adjusted to 2000	GDP at Constant Prices
2000	100,000	$1.50	$150,000	$1.50	$150,000
2005	150,000	$2.00	$300,000	$1.50	$225,000
2010	200,000	$3.00	$600,000	$1.50	$300,000

Labor Productivity

The measurement of the number of items produced per worker is called *productivity*. An increase in productivity is an important source of economic growth. Improvements in the quality of capital equipment, worker training, and management techniques can result in greater output from the same number of workers.

In a simple model, productivity is computed by dividing the *output* (the number of units produced) by the *input* (the number of hours worked). For instance, if Technoland's workforce produced 4,000 units of Techlatts in a total of 80 worker hours, productivity per worker would be 50 per hour.

$$\text{Productivity} = \frac{\text{Number of units produced (output)}}{\text{Number of hours worked (input)}}$$

$$\text{Productivity} = \frac{4,000 \text{ units}}{80 \text{ hours}} = 50$$

With additional training and/or improvement in equipment, the productivity figure would be expected to increase.

Worker productivity is the productivity of one worker. Worker productivity varies from one worker to another and is a measure of an individual worker's performance.

Inflation and Deflation

A sustained increase in the general level of prices for goods and services is called *inflation*. A controlled, general rate of inflation is one of the goals of governments. A moderate increase in prices and wages is a sign of a healthy, growing economy.

Business Math Connection

Using the formula for production, calculate the worker productivity for each Technoland worker in the table below to determine which worker's performance is the best.

PRODUCTIVITY BEFORE TRAINING		
Worker	Hours Worked	Units Produced
Alex	20	700
Maria	30	900
Natasha	20	400

SOLUTION
The formula for calculating productivity is

$$\text{Productivity} = \frac{\text{Number of units produced (output)}}{\text{Number of hours worked (input)}}$$

$$\text{Alex's productivity} = \frac{700}{20} = 35$$

$$\text{Maria's productivity} = \frac{900}{30} = 30$$

$$\text{Natasha's productivity} = \frac{400}{20} = 20$$

Inflation can be a problem if it increases too rapidly. There have been periods of time when our country has had very high rates of inflation. Government, businesses, and individuals continued to increase their spending, and prices continued to rise. Even though wages—the price paid for labor—increase during inflation, prices of goods and services often rise faster, so workers never catch up.

Comparing the relative value of wages and prices of one year with another is difficult because of inflation. For instance, in the early 1900s, eggs cost 14 cents per dozen, sugar cost 4 cents per pound, and coffee was only 15 cents per pound. Sound good? Well, at the same time, the average worker in our country earned 20 cents per hour, so the buying power of wages was low.

The opposite of inflation is deflation. *Deflation* is a sustained decrease in the general level of prices for goods and services. It usually occurs during a period when the economy is not doing well and workers are being laid off. Prices of products decrease, but people have less money to buy them. The most notable deflationary period in our country was during the Great Depression of the 1930s. Between 1929 and 1933, prices dropped about 25 percent. But people definitely were not better off. They could not afford to buy things even at the much lower prices.

CheckPOINT

Give a brief description of the three ways to measure the health of an economy.

_____

_____

TEAMWORK

To analyze the business cycle, divide into four teams. Each group should select one phase of the business cycle and discuss what effect that phase would have on team members' present lives. Then meet as a class and exchange the results of each of the team's discussions. Conclude by deciding which phase has the greatest effect on students and their families.

The Business Cycle

When people talk about the economy, they speak about good times and bad times. They discuss prices, new businesses, and new job creation. They also discuss businesses that close and jobs that are lost. Changes in the economy impact peoples' lives. Over the decades, economists have learned that an economy has ups and downs, good times and bad.

The movement of the economy from one condition to another and back again is called a **business cycle**. Business cycles are the recurring ups and downs of GDP. Business cycles have four phases: prosperity, recession, depression, and recovery.

Prosperity

At the high point of the business cycle, consumers enjoy prosperity. *Prosperity* is the phase where most people who want to work are employed and businesses produce goods and services in record numbers. Wages are good. The demand for goods and services is high. People are optimistic about the economy and feel good about themselves. Prosperity does not go on forever, however. Eventually the economy cools off and activity slows down.

Recession

An economy slowing down signals a recession. *Recession* is a phase of the business cycle where demand for goods and services begins to decrease, production decreases, unemployment begins to increase, and GDP growth slows down. This phase often means a decrease in sales for expensive goods, such as automobiles. When automobile companies cut back on production, businesses that supply steel, fabrics, and other goods needed in producing automobiles are affected. This ripple effect often causes smaller supply firms to go out of business. A decrease in the use of economic resources and a lower demand for goods and services signal this phase of the business cycle.

What is it about a recession that makes houses difficult to sell?

©3d brained, 2009/ Used under license from Shutterstock.com

Depression

If a recession gets worse and spreads throughout the economy, the result is depression. *Depression* is a phase of the business cycle marked by a prolonged period of unemployment, weak sales of goods and services, and business failures. GDP falls rapidly during a depression. During the Great Depression of the early 1930s, the unemployment rate reached 25 percent. Many people could not afford to provide for even their basic needs. Clothing and food were given out in "bread lines" at churches and charitable organizations. Depression described the emotional mood of the people as well.

Recovery

A welcome phase of the business cycle is known as recovery. *Recovery* is the phase in which unemployment begins to decrease, demand for goods and services begins to increase, and GDP begins to rise again. People are employed once again, and they buy more goods and services. When businesses begin to meet the increasing demand for their products, they hire more workers. More wages being earned increases demand for goods and services. Recovery leads an economy into the most-welcome business cycle, prosperity.

Check**POINT**

State what you consider to be the major characteristic of each of the four phases of the business cycle. Give reasons for your answer.

_____

_____

Think Critically

1. Why is it important to have a constant dollar GDP figure rather than one that just shows current prices? In what ways is GDP important to you?

_____

_____

_____

2. Why is moderate inflation good for the economy? Would it be desirable to have no inflation and no increase in prices or wages? Explain.

_____

_____

_____

3. What part of the business cycle is the U.S. economy in at the present time? What signs do you see that indicate this particular phase?

_____

_____

_____

Make Academic Connections

4. **Research** Find out about current inflation in countries around the world using Internet resources. Make a chart of the countries according to their inflation rates. How does the United States compare with other countries? Write a brief paragraph giving your thoughts about inflation worldwide.

5. **Business Math** Compute the worker productivity for each worker in the table below. Compare the results with the results for "productivity before training" in the Business Math Connection on page 19.

PRODUCTIVITY AFTER TRAINING			
Worker	Hours Worked	Units Produced	Productivity
Alex	15	750	_____
Maria	20	900	_____
Natasha	15	450	_____

Which worker had the most improvement in productivity?

_____

What does this exercise reveal about productivity?

_____

🌀 JUMP START

As business owners, Brianna and Brittney work hard in their business. Because they know that the business cycle will have an impact on their business, they spend time planning ahead. They want to succeed. To do that, they must determine the best price to charge for their cookies and the right number of cookies to bake. They have to gather information to use in making these decisions. What kinds of information do they need? What advice would you give them?

Economic Roles

All people share the economic roles of citizen, worker, and consumer. In performing these roles, you make decisions that affect both you and the entire economy. The interaction of supply and demand is an integral part of the economy. Your consumer role, as well as your citizen and worker role, affects our economy's supply and demand.

Your Citizen Role

Your citizen role is an important one. When you are old enough to vote, your political involvement will be important in your community. Keeping informed about the issues and the candidates running for office and then voting responsibly in elections is an important part of performing this role. Businesses and consumers are affected by those who hold political office and make decisions about what can and cannot be done in a community. By casting your vote, you help decide what actions to take as a community.

Helping to provide meals for the homeless, cleaning portions of a street or highway, or helping to raise money to build a new playground are examples of volunteer efforts by concerned citizens. These are examples of ways that you can perform your citizen role before you are of voting age. The way you perform your citizen role affects businesses and your community.

Your Worker Role

In your worker role in the economy, you are part of the process that supplies goods and services. Whether you process data on a computer, wait on customers, or design websites, you can supply an important good or service.

The wages you earn in your worker role allow you to buy things that you need and want, which in turn helps establish demand. In this way you find yourself on both sides of the buying and selling process. In your worker role, you have an opportunity to provide quality products and services. In your consumer role, you express your desire to buy products and services that are safe and reliable.

Your Consumer Role

As a consumer, you make decisions to buy or not to buy products and services. The United States is a market economy in which buyers and sellers in the marketplace are able to freely make decisions that affect the economy. These decisions, based on voluntary exchange in the marketplace, drive what will be produced. The buying decisions of all consumers—individuals, businesses, and governments—provide answers as to how our scarce resources will be used.

Individual buying decisions have a big influence on our economy. Individual consumers buy more than two-thirds of the goods and services produced.

Supply and Demand

When you make a decision to buy or not to buy certain goods and services, you are helping businesses make their decisions. Buying a good or service is sometimes called "casting your dollar vote." Your dollar vote tells a business, "I like this product or service, and I am willing to pay for it." When a business receives dollar votes, it receives information on the demand for its products.

Supply and Demand Relationships Demand is the relationship between the amount of a good or service that consumers are willing and able to buy and the price of the good or service. When a business knows the demand for its product, it can plan its production using whatever economic resources are needed. Demand is an important element in an economy.

Demand determines what supply businesses will provide. Supply is the amount of a good or service that businesses are willing and able to provide based on the price of the good or service. Suppliers will produce a good or service if it can be sold at a price that covers operating costs and yields a reasonable profit. Brianna and Brittney will sell cookies to stores for $8 a dozen if they can make a profit doing so. The number of those cookies that they bake depends on how many of those cookies the stores order. The stores place their orders based on how many of those cookies customers will buy at a price that allows the stores to make a reasonable profit. The stores' customers (consumers) establish the level of demand, and Brianna and Brittney are producers who provide the supply.

Supply and Demand Effect on Price As you can see, price is an important factor in doing business. A business must decide the best price to charge for its goods and services. Determining that price requires some good business decision making.

As the demand for a good or service increases, the price tends to go up. As demand begins to fall, the price generally goes down. Figuring out the right price at the right level of demand is something that a business must determine.

What do businesses do when there is low demand for a product?

A change in fashions or popular brands can cause some designer clothes to go out of style, resulting in lower demand. This causes their prices to drop. The new brands will be in high demand and will have higher prices. Consumers are willing to pay higher prices when they see value in their purchase and are not able to find a suitable alternative.

Supply also affects prices. When a product is in short supply, prices tend to increase if the demand stays the same. When the world demand for gasoline increases and the supply of crude oil is not increased or oil refineries do not produce more gasoline, prices at the pump go up rather quickly. When a drought or natural disaster affects the supply of coffee or vegetables, prices of those items may increase.

Other factors in the marketplace may be involved in setting prices as well. Prices may be high because the materials from which they are made are naturally scarce. Diamonds are a good example because they are found in only a few countries and in relatively small quantities. Because of their beauty and endurance, the demand for them is high. The price of a quality diamond has always been high.

CheckPOINT

List the three economic roles performed by individuals and give examples of what each role involves.

_____

_____

Your Economic Well-Being

How you perform your three economic roles also has an effect on the satisfaction you get from your life as an individual or family. Your well-being in the economy is referred to as your standard of living and your quality of life.

Standard of Living

The term *standard of living* refers to the way you live as measured by the kind and quantity of goods and services you can afford. You use your earnings to buy the things you need to maintain and improve your standard of living. The amount of money you have plus the decisions you make are major elements in determining your standard of living.

While you are a student, most of your needs and wants are met by your parents or guardian. Before long, however, you will be meeting your own needs and wants with the money you earn. Your success as a worker and good decisions in your consumer role will work together to determine your standard of living and your quality of life.

Quality of Life

Your *quality of life* is the satisfaction and enjoyment that you get from your life. Quality of life is not measured so much by the quantity of what you own and use but by the satisfaction that you get from your possessions and activities. For example, you can't put a price tag on the feelings you have while watching a beautiful sunset or the enjoyment you receive from hiking a trail or walking on a beach. Such things add an important dimension of satisfaction and enjoyment to life.

It is possible to have fewer goods and services than others and still have a high quality of life. In some lesser-developed economies, people have very few goods and services compared to what American citizens have. Yet visitors to such countries often are impressed with the satisfaction citizens of these countries show for their lives. The attitudes you have toward your possessions and your understanding of the difference between needs and wants affect your level of satisfaction with your quality of life.

CheckPOINT

Define standard of living and quality of life in your own words. Then make an observation about how you would rate both in your present life.

_____

_____

_____

Think Critically

1. Why is the consumer role so important in a market economy?

2. What is the difference between a dollar vote and a political vote? Which one, in your opinion, is more important?

3. Why is it important for businesses and consumers to understand how supply and demand affect an economy?

4. Why is it important to distinguish between standard of living and quality of life? Why are some people never satisfied with what they have?

Make Academic Connections

5. **Sociology** Make a list of some of the things that you have done over the past several weeks that relate to each of the three economic roles. Beside each item, indicate whether you were acting in your consumer, worker, or citizen role. What does this list tell you about your participation in the economy? Which economic role do you feel best prepared for? least prepared for? What are some things you can do to improve your participation in each of the three roles?

6. **Research** The Consumer Price Index (CPI) has figures that show changes in the level of prices over a period of time. Obtain information about the CPI through the library or Internet. Write a brief summary of what you learn about the U.S. economy at the present time. Are prices generally higher or lower than they have been in recent years?

Chapter Summary

1.1 **Market Economies**
  - A. All economic systems must solve the problem of scarcity in deciding what to produce, how to produce it, and for whom it is to be produced.
  - B. Market economies are characterized by private enterprise, private property, profit motive, and competition.

1.2 **Make Decisions**
  - A. Economies use natural, human, and capital resources by providing goods and services to meet the needs and wants of citizens.
  - B. Economic decision making is made most effective through the use of a six-step decision-making process.

1.3 **Healthy Economies**
  - A. GDP, labor productivity, and inflation/deflation are measurements that help to determine the health of an economy.
  - B. The phases of the business cycle are prosperity, recession, depression, and recovery.

1.4 **Participate in an Economy**
  - A. People perform three important roles as a citizen, worker, and consumer. These roles affect our economy's supply and demand.
  - B. Standard of living is measured by the goods and services you own. Quality of life means satisfaction you get from possessions and activities.

Vocabulary Builder

Choose the term that best fits the definition. Write the letter of the answer in the space provided. Some terms may not be used.

_____ 1. Things you must have to live

_____ 2. Relationship between the amount of a good or service that businesses are willing and able to provide and the price of the good or service

_____ 3. Total dollar value of goods and services produced by a country in one year

_____ 4. Cyclical movement of the economy from one phase to another

_____ 5. Conflict between unlimited wants and limited resources

_____ 6. Rivalry among businesses to sell their products and services

_____ 7. Relationship between the amount of a good or service that consumers are willing and able to buy and the price of the good or service

_____ 8. An economic system in which businesses and individuals are free to make their own decisions in the marketplace

_____ 9. A business's income minus its operating expenses

a. business cycle
b. capitalism
c. competition
d. demand
e. economic resources
f. goods
g. gross domestic product (GDP)
h. market economy
i. needs
j. profit
k. scarcity
l. services
m. supply
n. wants

Review Concepts

Point Your Browser

www.cengage.com/
school/business/21biz

10. What are the three questions that all economic systems must answer?

_____

_____

_____

11. What are the important characteristics of a market economy?

_____

_____

_____

12. Explain the difference between a need and a want.

_____

_____

_____

13. List the steps in the economic decision-making process.

_____

_____

_____

_____

14. What is meant by GDP?

_____

_____

_____

15. What is the difference between inflation and deflation? Which is more desirable in an economy? Explain why.

_____

_____

_____

_____

16. List the four phases of a business cycle.

_____

_____

17. How does consumer participation in an economy help determine supply, demand, and prices?

_____

_____

_____

18. In what ways is the worker role important?

_____

_____

_____

Apply What You Learned

19. Which of the three economic roles appeals to you the most? Give reasons for your answer.

_____

_____

_____

20. What would happen if everyone in each of your classes received exactly the same grade no matter what the individual did or did not do? How does this relate to the profit motive?

_____

_____

_____

21. How does supply and demand affect the price of a good or service?

_____

_____

22. Why do so many people not take the time to make decisions using a decision-making model? What might be the effect in the marketplace if more people did use it?

_____

_____

_____

23. Why is it important for you and others to understand the four phases of the business cycle?

_____

_____

_____

24. Explain how the three economic roles interact to affect standard of living and quality of life.

_____

_____

_____

_____

Make Academic Connections

25. **Environment** Protecting U.S. wetlands is important to the economy. Read articles or obtain information from the Internet on what is being done to preserve the wetlands. Find out why it is important to do so. Write a one-page report on your findings.

26. **Problem Solving** Scarcity is also a problem for individuals. Think back over your activities for the past several weeks. Identify some of the decisions you had to make that reflect the concept of scarcity of resources. Describe what you did to solve the problem of scarcity.

27. **Advertising** Read through several magazines and/or newspapers, noting what is contained in the advertisements. List five advertisements that describe goods and/or services. Explain what economic resources are involved in providing those goods and services.

28. **Government** Americans have many freedoms. These freedoms are important to you as an individual and to businesses. However, there are activities that you are not free to do. List one of the laws or regulations that protect others from harm or abuse but that limit our individual freedoms. Explain why this is necessary.

29. **Communication** The use of e-commerce, buying and selling over the Internet, is becoming more widespread. Based on your knowledge of online shopping, e-commerce, and what you learn through reading current articles, write a brief paper about how you think e-commerce and online shopping is affecting the marketplace. Consider questions such as the following:

    - How will the decision-making process be affected?
    - Are buying decisions too easy to make when shopping online?
    - Are online buying decisions being made too quickly?
    - Is it better to be able to see and handle merchandise before making a decision to buy?
    - What are the advantages and disadvantages of shopping online?

Ethical Dilemma

30. Jared would like to advertise his new product as "organic." However, he does not know the specific restrictions for labeling his product line as organic. Should he go ahead and advertise it as organic while he does more research about his product's ingredients to learn whether it is acceptable to market them as organic? He needs to get his product on the market quickly to beat his competitors. He believes that he can sell his product for a higher price if he markets it as organic. What advice do you have for Jared? What are the ethical issues Jared should consider?

CHAPTER 2

Businesses in Our Economy

Careers in Business

LEVI STRAUSS & CO.

Levi Strauss & Company was founded in 1853 by immigrant Levi Strauss. The company manufactures and markets jeans and casual sportswear under the Levi's®, Dockers®, and Slates® brands. It is one of the world's largest brand-name marketers, with sales in more than 110 countries and about 10,000 employees.

Retail marketing assistants at Levi Strauss & Co. work with retail marketing managers to develop and put retail marketing plans into practice. Retail marketing assistants also help organize retail advertising, promotions, and special events.

For this position, Levi Strauss & Co. wants people who have a bachelor's degree in business, marketing, or merchandising and three to five years of sales or marketing experience in retailing. The position calls for strong communication and analytical skills and experience giving computer-based presentations.

Think Critically

1. Levi Strauss & Co. focuses on brand building. How does the retail marketing assistant job relate to this brand focus?
2. Why do you think strong communication skills are needed in this position?

Project Objectives

- Identify businesses that operate in your area
- Research types of business ownership
- Research a marketing strategy

Photodisc/Getty Images

Getting Started

Read the Project Process below. Make a list of any materials you will need.

- Look at all the information you will gather for this project. Decide in your group how to put this information into a format that is easy to understand.
- Make a list of at least 20 different kinds of businesses that operate in your community, city, or state. Include both small and large businesses.

Project Process

2.1 Indicate whether each business on your list functions as a producer, intermediary, or service business. Be sure each type of business is represented. Does each business perform the six basic business activities?

2.2 Choose one business from each business category. Determine whether it is a sole proprietorship, partnership, corporation, franchise, cooperative, nonprofit corporation, joint venture, S corporation, or LLC. Discuss possible differences in the management of the various businesses.

2.3 Research a marketing strategy for one of your businesses. Can you identify the target market for your business? Which of the seven functions of marketing is the most important for your business? Why?

Chapter Review

Project Wrap-up Prepare a group presentation of the marketing strategy you researched. Include all the elements of a good marketing strategy.

Creatas Images/Jupiter Images

GOALS

Identify the three types of businesses

Describe the six business activities

KEY TERMS

extractors, p. 35

manufacturers, p. 35

intermediaries, p. 35

service business, p. 35

 JUMP START

Brianna and Brittney started their cookie business knowing that consumers would like their special cookies, and they were right—they are successful. They decide to expand their business by adding a line of cakes using a special recipe they developed with a honey base. They let customers taste samples of their cakes in stores, and the customers love them. Now with cookies and cakes to make and sell, they change the name of their expanded business to B&B Bakery. With a larger business, more employees, and more sales, it is even more important than before that Brianna and Brittney keep things running smoothly. What basic business activities must they perform to be successful?

©Izaokas Sapiro, 2009/ Used under license from Shutterstock.com

Types of Businesses

U.S. consumers buy goods and services from many kinds of businesses. You and your family might buy produce from farmers' markets or supermarkets and clothing from stores in shopping malls. You might buy a variety of merchandise over the Internet. You use the service of a computer repair store to repair your computer or printer. Businesses buy goods and services too. They buy products to resell, raw materials to use in producing products, and supplies to help them operate. Both consumers and businesses buy goods and services from three major types of businesses in our economy: producers, intermediaries, and service businesses.

Producers

Businesses that create products used by individuals and other businesses are called *producers*. If they take resources from nature to make their products or for direct consumption, they are referred to as **extractors**. Examples of extractors are oil refineries, coal and copper mines, and lumber mills. Farmers are another example because they cultivate land and use other natural resources to grow crops and raise livestock for consumption. A major group of producers is **manufacturers**, businesses who get supplies from other producers and convert them into their own products. Automobile companies are a good example of a manufacturer.

Many business activities start with products provided by producers. For instance, a builder gets started with lumber, equipment, and other materials to begin building a house. A computer company obtains a variety of components and parts from various manufacturers in order to assemble its computers.

Intermediaries

Businesses involved in selling the goods and services of producers to consumers and other businesses are referred to as **intermediaries**. They provide an important function in our economy. The most common types of intermediaries are retailers and wholesalers. A *retailer* sells products directly to consumers at a place of business. A *wholesaler* is an intermediary business that sells the products of a manufacturer or extractor to a retailer. Some intermediaries help in distributing and selling products and services. Specialized intermediaries include trucking companies, railroads, storage centers, advertising centers, sales offices, and data processing centers.

Service Businesses

Many businesses do not make products that we can see or handle. They offer something that is intangible, but that is nevertheless important. Instead of offering products for sale, a **service business** performs activities that are consumed by customers. Examples of typical service businesses include doctors, lawyers, accountants, painters, baby sitters, landscapers, dentists, and pet sitters. Types of service businesses that have emerged with the electronic age include web designers, Internet service providers, and online travel agents. Both businesses and consumers use service businesses.

DID YOU KNOW ?

In a recent year, it was reported that 60 percent of all U.S. employment was in service businesses.

CheckPOINT

Which type of business takes resources from nature to make its products? Name several examples.

_____

_____

TEAMWORK

Divide into three teams to identify businesses within the community (city, township, county, etc.) that are producers, intermediaries, or service businesses. Regroup as a class and compare the lists. How many businesses are commonly identified among the three teams? If there is a need to include additional businesses in any one of the categories, discuss this as a class.

Business Activities

A business must operate efficiently to stay profitable regardless of its size. One business might be large and complex and operate on a global basis while another is small and operates in just one community. Although there are many types and sizes of businesses, all must perform the following six basic business activities in order to be successful.

Generate Ideas

A business starts with a new idea for a product or a service. The idea could be a simple but new way to carry out an ongoing business process. It should improve what is being done and offer something that is better than what is available now. Competition in the marketplace demands that what is being offered is at least as good as or better than what the competition is offering. In that way, the consumer can select the best product or service for the best price. Research and development departments of large companies work full time to discover new products, services, and operating ideas. In small companies, managers keep abreast of new developments by reading trade publications and attending trade shows and seminars.

Raise Capital

The need for capital resources to operate a business is critical. This is especially true for small businesses. When the economy is in a downturn or a recession, it is often very difficult for small business entrepreneurs to obtain start-up capital. Governments at times offer stimulus packages or other incentives to help small businesses. Financial resources are needed to purchase buildings and equipment, hire and train employees, obtain licenses, and obtain items needed for day-to-day operations.

©Rob Marmion, 2009/ Used under license from Shutterstock.com

When are ideas likely to lead to successful products or services?

Tech Literacy

E-COMMERCE

Buying goods and services over the Internet is becoming a popular way of doing business. Companies are turning to e-commerce as a way of growing their businesses. As of 2009, an estimated quarter of the world's population, or approximately 1.5 billion, use the services of the Internet. E-commerce allows a business to have access to markets it otherwise would not enter, including markets in other countries. Developing company websites and making customer service a high priority are just two challenges that face businesses entering the online arena.

THINK CRITICALLY

How might the business activities for an e-commerce business differ from those of a traditional business?

The need for capital continues as a business becomes established, grows, and expands. Developing a good credit rating, a high-quality reputation, and a positive relationship with banks are important factors in raising future capital. Reinvesting profits in the business is also an excellent way to help the business grow. If there are investors in the business, maintaining a good relationship with them is important, as is attracting new investors.

Buy Goods and Services

Goods and services may be bought for resale or for use by a business. The owner of a men's clothing store, for instance, must buy shirts, slacks, suits, and coats to sell in the store. The store owner also needs a cash register, display cases, and other supplies. Examples of services that businesses purchase include advertising space in a newspaper or magazine and web page design.

Businesses that manufacture products must buy raw materials needed for their production process. Buying raw materials such as wheat, oil, plastic, steel, or chemicals is an important activity in operating a business. Manufacturers of automobiles purchase supplies such as tires, air bags, air conditioning units, batteries, and transmissions that are installed on the assembly lines.

Employ and Train Personnel

The most important resource for a business is people—it cannot operate without them. Except for one-person businesses, all businesses need to have a system for carrying out activities that attract, employ, and train employees. Human resources activities include recruiting, interviewing, and hiring employees. New employees receive training so that they perform their jobs correctly. Further training becomes necessary when procedures change, new tasks are added, or new technology is introduced.

Managing human resources requires knowledge of equal opportunity laws, health and safety regulations, and employee rights on issues such as promotions, transfers, layoffs, and firings. Except in very small businesses, these activities are carried out by a human resources department.

Market Goods and Services

Marketing activities are directed toward providing the kind of product or service consumers desire. Without good marketing, even the best products and services might not be known and, therefore, not purchased by consumers.

Many marketing activities begin before a product is produced and ready to sell. Marketers assist in designing and developing products based on what they learn about customers' needs and wants. Marketers have skills and knowledge on how to present the qualities of the products and services to the general public or to a specific target audience.

Why should marketers be involved in designing a product?

Maintain Business Records

All businesses must have some type of recordkeeping system so that owners and managers know the financial standing of the company. Computer technology is used extensively to produce a variety of reports useful in analyzing financial data related to the company's performance. The failure to keep adequate records is a major reason why some businesses fail.

Owners and managers need financial data and reports to track performance and make decisions. Customers need information about orders and payments. Governments require businesses to submit employment and other tax-related information. Computer programs help make recordkeeping easier and more accurate and also allow access to information on a timely basis.

CheckPOINT

Why is raising capital critical to the success of a business?

_____

_____

_____

Think Critically

1. If you were to start any one of the three types of businesses, and had access to all the resources needed, what kind would you start? Why?

_____

_____

2. What do you think are some of the reasons why service businesses are the fastest-growing sector of the economy?

_____

_____

3. Which activity that a human resources department performs do you think is the most important? Why?

_____

_____

4. If you were a business owner, what would you want to know about your business that could be provided by records? Make a list of those things.

_____

_____

Make Academic Connections

5. **Business Math** *Separation* refers to an employee who has left a business, whether the employee has quit or was fired. Employment records for three businesses are as follows: Gizmo Inc.: 700 employees, 56 separations; WidgeCo: 1,800 employees, 108 separations; Techno Builders: 1,200 employees, 78 separations. Calculate their employee turnover rate percentages. Why would these numbers be useful to human resource people?

   Turnover rate = Number of separations ÷ Number of employees

   Turnover rates: Gizmo Inc. _____ WidgeCo _____ Techno Builders _____

   Company with highest rate: _____ Lowest rate: _____

   _____

   _____

6. **Research** New businesses in a community bring many benefits. Employees spend their wages on new houses, furniture, and appliances to meet their everyday needs and wants. A business buys supplies and materials it needs. Find newspaper or magazine articles about a new business that recently opened in your community. How did the new business affect your community? Write a one-page report on your findings.

GOALS

Describe the nine forms of business ownership

Identify five business management activities

KEY TERMS

sole proprietorship, p. 40

partnership, p. 41

corporation, p. 42

board of directors, p. 42

franchise, p. 42

 JUMP START

The B&B Bakery continues to grow. Brianna and Brittney want to expand their business and open some new stores. They need to raise additional capital and have decided that the best way to do this is to take on a new partner. A business acquaintance has recommended a good friend, Emilio Torres, who has experience as an accountant and has worked as a legal assistant. After talking with him and learning that he has the funds to invest in their business, they agree to accept him as their partner. They believe that they can work together successfully. They now must decide how they will divide up five management activities among the three partners. What advice do you have for them?

©Tom Grill, 2009/ Used under license from Shutterstock.com

Forms of Business Ownership

In our economy, many thousands of people are business owners. How they run their business is not the same for every owner. Their form of business ownership affects how they operate their business, including how they make decisions, their sources of money, and their control over profits.

Common Forms of Business

There are three forms of business ownership that are most common in the business world—sole proprietorships, partnerships, and corporations. All three forms have advantages and disadvantages.

Sole Proprietorship A business owned and operated by just one person is called a **sole proprietorship**. Common examples are jewelry stores and

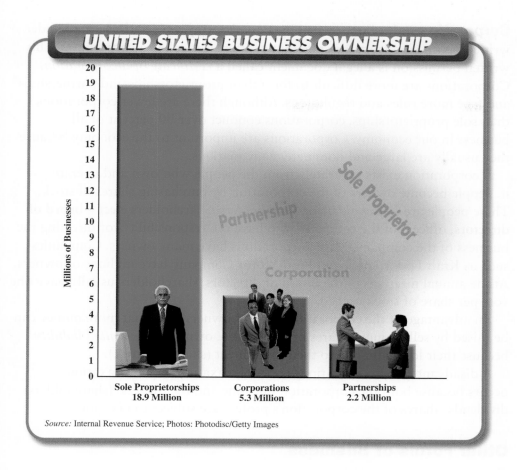

UNITED STATES BUSINESS OWNERSHIP

Millions of Businesses

20
19
18
17
16
15
14
13
12
11
10
9
8
7
6
5
4
3
2
1
0

Sole Proprietor
Partnership
Corporation

Sole Proprietorships
18.9 Million

Corporations
5.3 Million

Partnerships
2.2 Million

Source: Internal Revenue Service; Photos: Photodisc/Getty Images

restaurants. As the chart above shows, more than 70 percent of businesses in the U.S. economy have been operated as sole proprietorships. A sole proprietorship is the easiest form of business to start and end. There are few legal requirements that need to be met.

The sole proprietor has complete responsibility for all business decisions and management activities. In most cases, the owner also works in the business and may do many or all of the tasks. The sole proprietor keeps the profit but is also personally responsible for all debts of the business. If the business fails, the owner's personal assets may be claimed to pay off debts.

Partnership A business owned and managed by a small group—often not more than two or three people—who have entered into an agreement is called a **partnership**. Partnerships are also quite easy to start, but there will be a written document stating how the partners will share responsibilities. Having business partners often means having more money to invest in the business and more knowledge and expertise to run the business.

Partners may or may not be active in the business. Some partners may be *silent partners*, whose main role is to help finance the operation and give advice in certain areas of the business, while *active partners* run the day-to-day operations. An important part of the written partnership agreement is how profits will be shared. A disadvantage of a partnership is that partners have unlimited *liability*, or legal and financial responsibility, for the debts of the partnership. If the business fails and money is owed, each partner is liable for the entire debt.

TEAMWORK

Work with a partner. Reread the Jump Start feature and decide what to include in the partnership agreement. Assume that Emilio will invest an amount equal to what Brianna and Brittney have invested in the bakery. Have the groups share their recommendations for class discussion.

Corporation A business owned by a number of people and operated under written permission from the state that charters it is called a **corporation**. This written permission is a legal document called a *certificate of incorporation*. Corporations are more difficult to form than proprietorships and partnerships and face more rules and regulations. Although there are fewer corporations than sole proprietorships, corporations conduct over 70 percent of all business in our economy. Corporations are important to the economy because they usually are large and dominate many markets.

A corporation exists separately from the people who own and operate it. People become owners of the corporation by purchasing shares of stock. These people are *shareholders* or *stockholders*. Shareholders elect a **board of directors**, officers of the company who have the responsibility for directing the business of the company. Most corporations have many owners. Companies such as Kraft Foods, Intel, and Ford Motor Company have millions of owners. At the annual meetings of the board of directors, shareholders usually have one vote per share of stock owned.

An advantage of the corporation form of ownership is that more money can be raised by selling more shares of stock. Also, owners have *limited liability* because their loss is limited to their investment (shares of stock).

A disadvantage of corporations is double taxation. Double taxation occurs because both the corporation's income and the owners' (shareholders) dividends (shares of the corporation's profits) are subject to taxation.

Other Forms of Business

Although most businesses are organized as one of the three common forms of business already discussed, there are other specialized forms of business ownership from which to choose.

Franchises A **franchise** is a written contract granting permission to a businessperson to sell someone else's product or service. The contract spells out the duties and rights of the parties to the contract. The parties to the contract are the *franchisee*, the business owner who is buying the rights, and the *franchisor*, the parent company that grants the rights. Often included as part of the franchise agreement are the name of the business, the design and color of the building, the location of the business, and the uniforms of the employees. Franchises may be operated as sole proprietorships, partnerships, or corporations.

Franchises are a popular way of doing business. The franchisee maintains the daily operations and receives the profits of the business but must pay a franchise fee along with a percentage of the profits to the franchisor. Successful franchises include KFC, Wild Birds Unlimited, McDonalds, Jiffy Lube, Merry Maids, and Mail Boxes Etc.

NETBookmark

When it comes to owning a business, many people think buying a franchise is a good way to get started. There are many franchising opportunities available, but you should proceed cautiously before buying. Access www.cengage.com/school/business/21biz and click on the link for Chapter 2. What is the history of franchising? What are some of the advantages and disadvantages of owning a franchise? Why is it important to research a franchise before buying?

www.cengage.com/school/business/21biz

Cooperatives A business owned by the members it serves and managed in their interests is called a cooperative. There are two main types of cooperatives. In a *consumers' cooperative*, consumers buy goods and services together at lower prices than each person could buy individually. They also share in the cooperative's profits. A *producers' cooperative*, usually a farm organization, gives the producers greater bargaining power in selling their products and allows them to be more competitive in the marketplace.

A cooperative is much like a corporation. Its formation must be approved by the state. It may sell one or more shares of stock to each of its members. A board of directors may be chosen to direct the business. Profits earned may be refunded to members at the end of the business year. Part of the profit is normally kept for business expansion.

Nonprofit Corporation Corporations that are created for social, political, charitable, educational, or general welfare purposes are known as *nonprofit corporations*. Examples are private colleges and universities and agencies such as the YMCA and the American Red Cross. Nonprofit organizations provide a service, and earning a profit is not their primary goal. They are free from corporate income taxes and can receive grants and donations from individuals and businesses. As with other corporations, they must organize as a corporation, and the government must approve their purpose and operations. Nonprofits file annual reports to the government to maintain their nonprofit status.

You may live in an incorporated town. A *municipal corporation*, or *municipality*, is a nonprofit corporation that can operate much like a city but is not governed under a charter granted by the state. It levies taxes, passes rules and regulations, provides police and fire protection, and provides a variety of services for its citizens. Unlike a business corporation, no stock is issued and revenues are from taxes rather than profits.

Joint Ventures An agreement between two or more companies to share a business project is known as a *joint venture*. It is a type of partnership that includes sharing of profits, as well as sharing of control among the partners. This can include the sharing of raw materials, shipping facilities, management activities, and production facilities.

Manufacturing companies often find joint ventures to be useful. A good example is the joint venture between the Ford Motor Company and the Japanese Mazda Motor Corporation. Mazda produced parts that the Ford Motor Company used in its cars, and Mazda set up assembly plants for Ford Motor vehicles. Joint ventures between Japanese and U.S. automobile manufacturers have become common.

S Corporations Another type of business, *S corporations*, gets its name from a section of the Internal Revenue Service

Why are joint ventures a popular way of doing business?

code. Many small businesses favor this type of corporation. One advantage of the S Corporation is the elimination of double taxation. Under this form of organization, all income is passed through to the owners in the form of dividends and is taxed on their individual tax returns. The corporation's income is not taxed. An S corporation still offers shareholders the limited liability of a corporation, meaning their personal assets are separated from debts incurred by the business.

Limited Liability Company A kind of corporation that is worldwide, but relatively new in the United States, is a limited liability company (LLC). LLCs are allowed by state statutes and first appeared in the United States in 1977. By 1996, nearly all states had enacted a statute allowing the existence of LLCs. A national Uniform Limited Liability Company Act was adopted in 1996 and was revised in 2006.

A limited liability company (LLC) combines the best features of a corporation and a partnership. It provides liability protection for the owners but does not require a complex set of organizational and operating requirements such as those needed for a corporation. A simple set is all that is needed. Articles of incorporation or bylaws also are not required. Only a simple document, much like a partnership agreement, needs to be developed.

Manage a Successful Business

For a business to be successful, someone must plan, organize, staff, lead, and control its operations. Managers are responsible for performing or coordinating those activities. In a small business, the owner often performs all of these activities.

Plan

The process of thinking, gathering, and analyzing information, as well as making decisions about all phases of the business, is called *planning*. Goals and standards are set for the business, and strategies and measurements are established for achieving them. Some managers spend too much time on day-to-day operations and fail to spend enough time on planning. That is a problem in many businesses, but especially in sole proprietorships.

Organize

The process of determining what work has to be done and who is to do it is called *organizing*. An important part of organizing is assigning work to employees and observing employees as they perform their jobs. Responsibility is given to certain people to see that jobs are done correctly. In large businesses, *organization charts* are often drawn up to show worker relationships and lines of authority and responsibility.

Staff

Staffing includes the many activities involved in finding, selecting, hiring, training, evaluating, and rewarding employees. There are many laws and regulations regarding employees' rights that must be known and followed by all sizes of businesses. For example, the person responsible for interviewing potential employees must be aware of what can and cannot be asked in the interview. Employment agencies can be helpful in assisting small business owners in locating potential employees.

Lead

It is important that employees are directed in their work so that they perform their tasks correctly and in a timely manner. This activity is called *leading*. People should be guided to perform according to plans and procedures of the business so that the work that they do is productive. Effective leaders can inspire workers to perform work tasks efficiently and accept personal responsibility for achieving goals of the company. Good leaders make sure that their workers are recognized and rewarded for excellence.

Control

When managers or supervisors compare what has been accomplished with what was planned, they are engaging in the process known as *control*. This involves determining whether or not operations are proceeding as planned. Standards are set up in the planning stage, and measurements are determined to track whether or not the standards are met. For instance, a business might set a standard for employees to handle 12 customer-inquiry calls per hour. The control factor would be to know the actual number of calls handled per hour by each worker. Control is directly related to planning.

CheckPOINT

What activities do managers perform during the planning process?

_____

_____

_____

Think Critically

1. Why do you think there are so many sole proprietorships in the U.S. economy?

_____

_____

2. What are some of the advantages of operating a business as a franchise rather than just going into business on your own?

_____

_____

_____

3. Which of the five key management activities do you think would be the most challenging for you to perform? Why?

_____

_____

_____

4. How are the business activities of controlling and planning related?

_____

_____

Make Academic Connections

5. **Communication** As a business owner, you must realize that when you speak, what you say is only part of the message you convey. For instance, in U.S. culture, lack of eye contact suggests that the listener is not interested in what the speaker is saying. Research nonverbal speech or body language. Describe two examples of nonverbal communication.

6. **Problem Solving** Jamie Andrews has operated a successful one-person furniture business for 25 years. He takes pride in his work and enjoys his business, but he does not like the long hours required of him as the owner-manager. A reputable furniture manufacturer has offered to take over his line of furniture at a very good price. Jamie's financial future would be secure, but he would no longer have total control over how to build his line of furniture. Write two paragraphs, one explaining the positive points and one explaining the negative points of this arrangement. Next, write a paragraph with your recommendation.

7. **Technology** Design a website for B&B Bakery. Include bakery goods and services they offer and any special seasonal offerings. Present your website in class.

JUMP START

Brianna, Brittney, and Emilio decide to rename their bakery. They are now The Triad Bakery. To keep their business growing, they decide to develop a formal marketing strategy. The target market for their products includes heads of households—people who buy bakery goods for their families. Three basic marketing objectives they set for the next 12 months are (1) to get 40 percent of all households in the community to try a cookie or cake from their bakery, (2) to obtain 20 percent of the market for fresh-baked cakes and cookies, and (3) to achieve net sales of $250,000. Given their target market and these marketing objectives, describe each element of the marketing strategy you would recommend for the Triad Bakery.

GOALS

Explain what marketing involves

Identify the functions of marketing

KEY TERMS

marketing strategy, p. 48

target market, p. 48

marketing orientation, p. 48

channel of distribution, p. 49

markup, p. 52

©Zsolt Nyulaszi, 2009/ Used under license from Shutterstock.com

Marketing Basics

Marketing is the process of informing the general public about goods and services that are available for sale at a convenient location or online. Marketing is an important part of doing business. If potential customers don't know about a business's products or services, who will buy these items?

All businesses get involved in developing a marketing strategy in one way or another. In developing the marketing strategy, businesses must identify their target market, consider the needs and wants of customers when planning their product or service, determine what price to charge, promote the product or service, and plan the channels of distribution.

Marketing Strategy

The plan that a company develops to show how it will use marketing to achieve its goals is called its **marketing strategy**. In developing the marketing strategy, marketers must decide whose needs or wants the business will try to satisfy and then develop a marketing mix to satisfy those needs and wants.

Target Market Marketers must identify a group of consumers whose needs or wants can be satisfied by the business's products or services. A group of individuals or businesses that has similar product needs is called a **target market**.

In the area of food service, for example, different retailers have identified different target markets. If a restaurant's target market is families who have young children, it may feature special meals for children and may have playgrounds. Other restaurants target an adult market and may have a more upscale interior and offer menus that appeal to this clientele.

Marketing Mix A second step in developing marketing strategy is to create a marketing mix. A *marketing mix* involves a blend of four elements: product, distribution, price, and promotion. A business must make many decisions to ensure that a product's benefits are communicated to customers and that the product is available in the location and at the price that meets the customers' needs. The right marketing mix can result in a profitable business.

Marketing Orientation

Businesses that have a **marketing orientation** consider the needs of customers when developing products and services. Businesses cannot assume that they know everything about what potential customers want. As they seek new markets, businesses conduct research studies to determine consumers' desires

Cross-Cultural Relationships

CULTURE AND BUYING DECISIONS

Companies sell to consumers in other countries to expand business opportunities. To achieve success in other countries, the company must consider the cultures in those countries. Culture is the sum of a country's way of life, and it influences consumers' buying decisions. In some Southeast Asian countries, for example, toothpaste that claims users will have "whiter teeth" may not sell well. This is because people there chew areca nuts wrapped in betel leaves, which turn teeth red/orange, and this is considered an attractive side effect.

Think Critically

Why is the culture of a country such an important consideration for international marketers?

for goods and services, their ability and willingness to pay for those goods and services, and other factors that affect their potential as future customers. A business might have researchers on staff, or it may employ research companies to do this research for it. The results of the research are used in designing a product or service that will meet the desires identified by consumers.

Marketing Channels

When a product or service is ready for market, it must be made available. Few products are sold directly by the producer to the consumer. The path that a product travels as it goes from producer to consumer is called a **channel of distribution**. There are two basic channels of distribution, direct and indirect.

A *direct channel* brings the product to the consumer directly from the producer. Farm products are among those that are marketed in this channel through roadside stands and farmers' markets. Some manufacturers of household goods, such as cosmetics and kitchen products, market their products through direct selling as well.

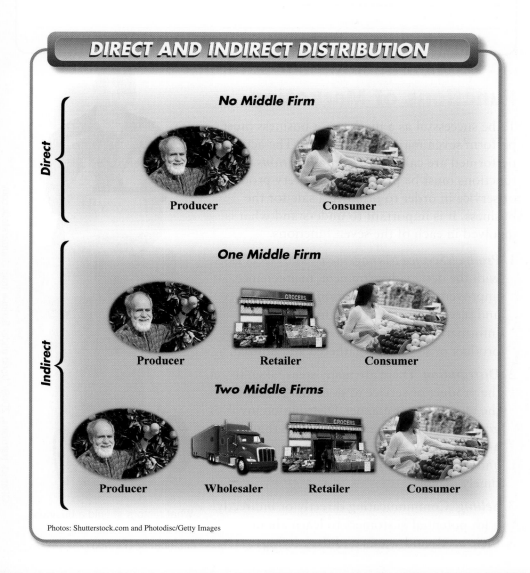

DIRECT AND INDIRECT DISTRIBUTION

Direct

No Middle Firm

Producer   Consumer

Indirect

One Middle Firm

Producer   Retailer   Consumer

Two Middle Firms

Producer   Wholesaler   Retailer   Consumer

Photos: Shutterstock.com and Photodisc/Getty Images

However, most products go through an *indirect channel* of distribution. The indirect channel consists of one or more businesses that come between the producer and the consumer. These middle businesses, intermediaries, are necessary for the marketing functions to be completed.

A wholesaler often buys large quantities of a product and breaks them down into smaller quantities that are suitable for retailers to sell to consumers. Wholesalers also store and transport products. A retailer then sells products directly to consumers at a place of business. The retailer gets many different products from wholesalers, displays them, and makes it convenient for consumers to shop and make purchases. Shopping malls are popular because they bring together a variety of retailers in one place, making shopping even more convenient for consumers.

CheckPOINT

In what ways does a wholesaler provide a service to a retailer?

_____

_____

Functions of Marketing

To be successful as a marketer, a business must perform seven marketing activities. The activities performed are called *marketing functions*. These functions must be performed for every product or service in order to produce a sale for the business. It is important to understand what is involved in each of the seven functions.

1. *Product/Service Management* Marketers assist with the design, development, maintenance, improvement, and acquisition of products and services that meet consumer needs. Information and test results related to a new product or service are gathered and utilized.

2. *Distribution* There are many steps taken to get the product or service to potential customers in the most efficient manner. Distribution involves giving careful consideration to such things as shipping, handling, and storing products and getting them to the desired locations in a timely manner.

3. *Selling* Communicating directly or indirectly with potential customers to learn about their needs and wants and then trying

What factors should a business consider when choosing a distribution method?

FUNCTIONS OF MARKETING

- MARKETING-INFORMATION MANAGEMENT
- SELLING
- FINANCIAL ANALYSIS
- DISTRIBUTION
- PRICING
- PRODUCT/SERVICE MANAGEMENT
- PROMOTION

to satisfy those needs and wants is part of the selling function. When a salesperson meets face-to-face with a potential customer and discusses the customer's desires and the features of the product or service, it is a direct sale. It is indirect when it is sold through e-commerce, telemarketing, videoconferencing, or instant messaging. Whatever mode is used, it is important that the message is clear and understood by the seller and the buyer so that the transaction can be made successfully.

4. *Marketing-Information Management* Important marketing decisions must be based on reliable information, such as information about the target market and customer needs. This information can come from a company's own customers or from more generalized data. The gathering and using of marketing data is important because it can be used to improve decision making. Computer technology and the Internet are important in the management and gathering of data needed for this function, especially when global markets are involved.

5. *Financial Analysis* A business must budget to support the purchase of products and services needed to produce and market the products or services it sells. Customers must have the resources and methods to pay for their purchases, so a business may offer financing options for its customers and assist them in finding the best way to handle their payments. Businesses must be paid in a timely manner to meet their expenses and continue to operate.

6. *Pricing* This process sets and communicates the value of products and services through an established price. Consumers want to know that they are getting a fair value for the money they are spending. Setting a price too low may cause a business to lose money. Setting a price too high may cause

Business Math Connection

A retail clothing store purchases a shirt for $25 from the manufacturer. The retailer plans to sell the shirt to consumers for $45. Calculate the markup and rate of markup.

SOLUTION

To calculate the markup, subtract the cost from the selling price.

Markup = Selling price − Cost
Markup = $45 − $25
Markup = $20

To calculate the rate of markup as a percentage of cost, divide the markup by the cost.

Rate of markup = Markup ÷ Cost
Rate of markup = $20 ÷ $25
Rate of markup = 0.8 = 80%

customers to buy a competitor's product or service. There are three goals of pricing: (1) to cover costs and generate a profit, (2) to set a price that consumers will consider to be a good value, and (3) to be competitive. The amount that is added to the cost of producing a product or service is called a **markup**.

7. *Promotion* Marketers search for effective ways to communicate with consumers and encourage the purchase of their goods and services. Advertising and other promotional methods have to compete with those of competitors, which often challenges the creativity of marketers. Many forms of advertising appear in newspapers, magazines, and other print media. In addition, other methods, such as radio, television, the Internet, contests, product displays, and sponsorships, are used to expose a business and its products to the public. One of the main goals of promotion is to communicate the advantages and benefits of a business's products and services.

TEAMWORK

As a team, identify a new product that could be put on the market. Then brainstorm ideas for promoting the product.

CheckPOINT

Name and give examples of two marketing functions.

_____

_____

_____

Think Critically

1. Explain why it is important for all businesses to be aware of the importance of marketing and what it involves.

_____

_____

_____

2. How do middle businesses (intermediaries) in an indirect channel of distribution benefit consumers?

_____

_____

_____

3. Which of the three goals of pricing do you think has the needs of the consumer most in mind? Explain your answer.

_____

_____

_____

4. Do you think there should be some controls on the amount businesses can mark up their goods and services? Why or why not?

_____

_____

_____

_____

Make Academic Connections

5. **Business Math** Calculate the markups, rates of markup as a percentage of cost, and selling prices for the missing items in the chart below. In working this problem, be careful that your decimal points are correct.

Item	Cost	Markup	Rate of Markup	Selling Price
A	$50	$5	_____	_____
B	$66	_____	33%	_____
C	$15	$2.75	_____	_____
D	$110	_____	4%	_____
E	$6	$0.90	_____	_____

6. **Advertising** Select several advertisements from magazines and newspapers that interest you. Make a list of product features that are emphasized in the advertisements. Then describe the basic appeal of the advertisement. Does it appeal to you based on price, features, or ability to meet a need or want? Organize this information into a spreadsheet.

Chapter Summary

2.1 **Business Activities**
- **A.** Businesses are classified as producers, intermediaries, or service businesses.
- **B.** Businesses must generate ideas, raise capital, buy goods and services, employ and train personnel, market goods and services, and maintain records.

2.2 **Business Ownership**
- **A.** The most common forms of business ownership are sole proprietorships, partnerships, and corporations. Specialized forms of business ownership include franchises, cooperatives, nonprofit corporations, joint ventures, S corporations, and limited liability companies.
- **B.** Business owners engage in planning, organizing, staffing, leading, and controlling their businesses.

2.3 **Effective Marketing**
- **A.** Marketing is the process of informing the general public about a business's goods and services. Businesses must create a marketing strategy, use a marketing orientation, and develop marketing channels to achieve its marketing goals.
- **B.** The seven functions of marketing are product/service management, distribution, selling, marketing-information management, financial analysis, pricing, and promotion.

Vocabulary Builder

Choose the term that best fits the definition. Write the letter of the answer in the space provided. Some terms may not be used.

_____ 1. Business owned and operated by one person		**a.** board of directors
_____ 2. Officers of a company who direct the business of the company		**b.** channel of distribution
_____ 3. The amount added to the cost of producing a product or service		**c.** corporation
_____ 4. A written contract granting permission to sell someone else's product		**d.** extractors
_____ 5. Group of individuals or businesses that have similar product needs		**e.** franchise
_____ 6. The plan that shows how a business will use marketing to achieve its goals		**f.** intermediaries
		g. manufacturers
_____ 7. Businesses that get products from other producers and convert them into their own products		**h.** marketing orientation
_____ 8. Considering the needs of customers when developing a product or service		**i.** marketing strategy
		j. markup
_____ 9. Business owned and operated by a small group who have entered into an agreement		**k.** partnership
		l. service business
_____10. The path that a product travels as it goes from producer to consumer		**m.** sole proprietorship
		n. target market

Review Concepts

Point Your
Browser
www.cengage.com/
school/business/21biz

11. How are extractors important to the U.S. economy?

_____

_____

_____

12. Explain how a service business might help another business.

_____

_____

_____

13. What is the most important resource for a business? What are some things that are involved in managing that resource?

_____

_____

_____

14. Why do businesses need to keep records?

_____

_____

15. How can you become an owner of a corporation?

_____

_____

16. What are some examples of nonprofit corporations?

_____

_____

17. Who owns a cooperative and what is done with its profits?

_____

_____

_____

18. What six business activities must all businesses perform?

_____

_____

19. What five management activities must all businesses perform?

_____

_____

20. What is a channel of distribution?

_____

_____

21. What are marketing functions?

_____

_____

22. Distinguish between direct and indirect selling.

_____

_____

_____

Apply What You Learned

23. If you were in business for yourself and had to add a partner to help finance an expansion, what are some traits or characteristics that you would look for in a partner in addition to his or her finances?

_____

_____

_____

_____

24. You own 500 shares of the stock in the C-D-E Corporation and have one vote for each share of stock you own. If you are only one of hundreds of thousands of shareholders, why would you want to attend the annual shareholders' meeting?

_____

_____

_____

_____

25. Why are intermediaries needed in the channels of distribution? What are some functions they perform that are of value to you?

_____

_____

_____

_____

26. Why is it important to set the right price for a product or service? What are the consequences of setting a price that is too low or too high?

_____

_____

_____

_____

Make Academic Connections

27. **Economics** Make a list of five different kinds of service businesses in your community and note briefly the services that they provide. Then write a paragraph about what impact there would be on your community's economy if these businesses were not in operation. What inconveniences or additional costs would be involved for businesses and consumers?

28. **Consumer Economics** Marketing businesses are said to add value to a product through the services they offer in moving the product from the manufacturer to the consumer. Make a list of five products that you buy or use. Consider what value has been added to them by marketing services. For each product, describe the ways in which value is added.

29. **Technology** In the U.S. economy, new technology for heavy machinery is used by farmers, road builders, construction companies and manufacturers. Use Internet resources to find information about some of the heavy machinery being used or marketed today. Find out as much as you can about how much work these machines can do compared with older equipment and machines. Write a paragraph explaining your findings.

30. **Business Math** Calculate the markups, rates of markup as a percentage of cost, and selling prices for the missing items in the chart below. In working this problem, be careful that your decimal points are correct.

Item	Cost	Markup	Rate of Markup	Selling Price
A	$4.50	_____	9%	_____
B	$12	$4	_____	_____
C	$85		18%	_____
D	$250	$110	_____	_____
E	$49	_____	21%	

31. **Creative Writing and Art** Create a full-page advertisement for the Triad Bakery that would appeal to the person who buys bakery goods for a family. Your ad should fulfill the basics of a good marketing strategy.

Ethical Dilemma

32. At her pet shop, Reyna sells a unique toy made in a factory in a foreign country. That country has been in the news recently because of its child labor practices. Reyna pays higher labor costs to ensure that her pet toys are made of high quality using safe practices with no child labor. However, she fears that if her customers know where the toy is made, they will not buy it. To counteract this, she decides not to identify the country of manufacture on the tag and instead lists the factory certification number. Is Reyna misleading her customers? If so, how? If not, why? How else could she handle her dilemma?

Business Management and Leadership

Careers in Business

APPLIED TECH SOLUTIONS, INC.

Applied Tech is a small business headquartered in Madison, Wisconsin. It is an Information Technology (IT) provider that focuses on meeting the IT needs of small to medium-sized businesses. It has 22 employees, including 12 technicians.

Applied Tech has an initiative to help small business owners with green "makeovers." The Network Operations Center (NOC) Technician provides support to clients on technical and green issues. NOC technical staff can assist customers in identifying and implementing products and systems that are green-friendly and minimize electricity usage. They also assist in the professional removal and recycling of electronic waste. The technicians provide proactive and reactive support for their clients on technical and green issues.

NOC technicians need at least a two-year Associates degree in a business or computer-related field and two to three years of related experience in infrastructure/network and/or help desk environments.

Think Critically

1. Why is the green-friendly service offered by Applied Tech needed?
2. What does it mean to be proactive or reactive?

Project Objectives

- Write a business plan
- Make decisions appropriate for the business
- Evaluate the business plan to make sure it is complete and realistic

©Svetlana Turilova, 2009/ Used under license from Shutterstock.com

Getting Started

Read the Project Process below. Make a list of any materials you will need.

- Your group will write a business plan for a business that will grow and sell roses wholesale to florists. The goal is to provide roses that are superior to other competing businesses in town. Services will include cut flowers and potted rose plants. The owner has experience from a local nursery. (Alternatively, select another type of business.)
- As a group, name the business and plan its operations. Make any assumptions you need to complete the operating and business plans.

Project Process

3.1 Review the parts of a business plan. Analyze the market for roses in your area. (Alternatively, perform this analysis on the other product selected.)

3.2 Discuss the leadership traits the owner of your business will need.

3.3 Decide whether the owner will need to hire employees. Plan compensation and benefits for the owner and his or her employees.

3.4 Develop a budget. Decide what kind of equipment to purchase, how much start-up capital will be needed, and how to obtain the capital.

Chapter Review

Project Wrap-up Draw up a formal business plan based on the group's analysis. As a class, review and discuss each group's business plan. What are the strengths and weaknesses of each? Is each business plan complete?

©gemphotography, 2009/ Used under license from Shutterstock.com

JUMP START

Brianna and Brittney started their business because they liked to bake cookies and they were good at it. They liked being independent and did not mind working long hours. Before starting the business, Brittney attended a small business owner's seminar conducted by the Small Business Administration, and Brianna worked in a supermarket's baked goods department, which gave her insight into customers' likes and dislikes. What they failed to do before starting their business, however, was to write a business plan. Although their business has been successful, they now want to grow it. But without a business plan, they have no direction on where they want the business to go and how to get there. With Emilio as their partner, they decide it is time to prepare a business plan. How should they begin the process of writing their business plan?

Photodisc/Getty Images

Small Businesses

A **small business** is an independent business with fewer than 500 employees. The greatest percentage of businesses in the United States are small businesses, and they employ half of all private sector employees. In a recent year, there were approximately 28 million U.S. small businesses. Small businesses play a vital role in our economy.

Meeting Customer Needs

Small businesses often serve customers when the number of products needed in a market is too small for a larger business to produce or sell profitably. The requirements of a market might also be so specialized that a small business can handle the need more efficiently. It is often possible for a small business to adapt its business to meet the precise needs of customers because its organization has the flexibility to adjust more easily to meet individual needs.

Small businesses generally serve fewer customers and have more personal contact with customers than do larger companies. They also tend to distribute and service their own products. Small businesses usually get direct information from their customers about their likes and dislikes.

Small businesses are especially suited to providing unique services for customers. They may plan a wedding or design a customized sound system for a home. Small business representatives tend to take special interest in serving their customers.

How do small businesses have an advantage over larger businesses?

©Monkey Business Images, 2009/ Used under license from Shutterstock.com

A big business has a clear advantage when a large number of customers are willing to buy standard products and services and prefer low-cost, efficient delivery. Small businesses gain the advantage when customers have unique needs, want more individual attention, and are willing to pay more for the product or service to obtain what they really want. Customers generally see small businesses as really caring about and providing what they want.

Starting a Small Business

Have you ever thought about going into business for yourself? Many people have, but not many actually follow through on their desire. Before starting a business, you need to determine if you possess the characteristics needed to succeed.

Characteristics of Small Business Owners Those who start businesses find that they work long hours and have many management tasks to perform. However, they are willing to do this since it allows them to perform the kind of work that they enjoy and to be in charge of their own business.

Characteristics of men and women who are successful small business owners have been studied and analyzed. These studies have found that successful small business owners tend to be independent, persistent, and self-motivated. They like doing things themselves, they stay with a task until it is completed, and they do not need someone to supervise them to get a job completed.

TEAMWORK

Consider some innovative ideas or activities that you like to do that could lead to an income-producing business. Make a list of what you identify. Then divide into small groups and discuss what you would need to get one or more of the businesses started successfully. Share answers with the class.

Successful owners are also energetic and willing to do what it takes to make their own business a success. They must also be risk takers and cannot be afraid to make mistakes. Mistakes should be viewed as learning experiences.

Ideas New small business ideas can come from many sources. A common source is a hobby or an activity the owner enjoys doing. Personal interests and related business experience can both be important. Ideas can come from magazines, websites, and other media. It is important to conduct research to decide if the hobby or activity can be made into a profitable business.

Acting on an idea is the next important step. Finding the right location is a very important consideration. If you want your customers to come to you, your business should be easy to find. If you will be producing a product, you should be near the source of materials and shipping points. Timing is another important factor. If your product or service is seasonal, you will need to begin your business at a favorable time of the year.

Why is it important to conduct research before starting a business?

Preparation and Research Putting your idea into action requires preparation and research. Preparation includes obtaining information about your product or service and your competition. Time spent at the beginning gathering information from books, seminars, magazines, and other businesses will help you avoid problems later. It is good to study as much information as possible to help assure that decisions are based on the best data available.

Information gathered should include potential customers, competition, relevant government regulations, and local ordinances and requirements. Sources of information include the Internet, government offices, local libraries, and the Small Business Administration.

The **Small Business Administration (SBA)** is a government agency that provides services and helpful publications to small businesses. The SBA works through small business assistance centers, often in cooperation with local colleges and universities. The SBA provides special assistance for minority-owned small businesses. Another source of help is the Service Corps of Retired Executives (SCORE), an SBA-sponsored group that offers free advice and consultation to small business owners from retired executives with a wide array of business backgrounds.

Small Business Problems

The failure rate for small businesses is quite high. The reasons for failure are varied, but the following are the most common.

- Not keeping adequate records
- Not having enough start-up money

- Having a poor location
- Lacking management experience or experience with the type of business being managed
- Not controlling business expenses or managing credit to customers
- Failing to have a business plan

These reasons for failure can be avoided or overcome by careful management and thorough education. The development of a business plan is a major step in the direction of helping to assure a successful small business.

CheckPOINT

What are some characteristics of successful small business owners?

_____

_____

The Business Plan

When successful small businesses are compared to those that fail, one thing stands out—the successful businesses developed and followed a business plan. All major activities and management functions are included in the plan. Key elements of a business plan are shown in the box below.

KEY ELEMENTS OF A BUSINESS PLAN

Description of the Business
- the business idea
- major products and services
- ownership structure
- owner's qualifications
- strengths and weaknesses
- long- and short-term goals

Description of the Competition
- industry characteristics
- condition of the economy
- strengths and weaknesses of competitors

Marketing Plan
- description of marketing activities
- description of resources needed
- schedule of marketing activities

Customer Analysis
- description of customers
- location, number, and resources of customers
- sales forecasts

Operations Plan
- organization of the company
- description of major operations
- analysis of resources needed
- human resource plans

Financial Plan
- start-up costs
- long- and short-term financial needs
- sources of financing
- budgets and financial statements

What Is a Business Plan?

A **business plan** is a written description of the business idea and how it will be carried out, including all major activities. There are key features that include a general description of the company, the owner's qualifications, a description of the product or service, an analysis of the market (demand, customers, and competition), and a financial plan.

Most business plans are developed for one year and updated the next year. The business plan is especially important if the business owner needs help from others and is usually required if financing is needed.

By developing a business plan, the owner is forced to think about important activities, the time they take, and their cost. Potential problems may be identified. The plan helps keep the business on its mission to success. It can be used as a tool for managing the business.

How can a business plan help a business owner succeed?

©Haywiremedia, 2009/ Used under license from Shutterstock.com

Developing a Business Plan

The business owner is responsible for developing the business plan. A well-developed plan will lay out an idea, require an owner to analyze her or his concept, and make decisions about key business activities such as production, marketing, staffing, and financing.

Tech Literacy

TECHNOLOGY TOOLS

When it comes to creating a business plan, help is available on the Internet. A quick search using the keywords "business plan template" or "business plan sample," finds numerous matches. A template allows you to plug in specific information to create a professional-looking business plan.

THINK CRITICALLY

What do you see as some advantages and disadvantages of using a business plan template?

Why is it best to have another person review your business plan?

Some owners may hire someone to write the plan, while others will get help from a local bank or the Small Business Administration. In either case, the owner must be familiar with all of the information and make the major decisions for the plan.

After outlining the key elements of the business plan, additional information that is needed must be gathered and reviewed. Reviewing the information is important, and the owner might do this or may get help in doing it. A bank or local office of the SBA can provide assistance. Any decisions made based on the review, however, should be made by the small business owner. The owner should also review and study other business plans and study information on the activities and performance of similar businesses, especially those that could be potential competitors.

The owner should also develop strategic alternatives, including plans for adjusting production, marketing, staffing, and financing if needed. The owner then needs to select the best choices from the alternatives.

Each section of the business plan must be written out in a careful and detailed manner. Before the plan is completed and ready to be used, it is a good idea for the owner to have at least one business professional review the plan and offer advice about its strengths and weaknesses. When the business plan is complete, the owner will have a management plan ready to guide his or her business to success.

CheckPOINT

What are an owner's responsibilities in developing a business plan?

_____

_____

Think Critically

1. Which characteristics of a successful small business owner do you think are most important to the success of the business? Why?

_____

_____

2. Why do you think hobbies or activities someone likes to do are often the beginning of a small business enterprise?

_____

_____

3. Which element of the business plan do you believe to be most critical? Why?

_____

_____

_____

4. Why is a business plan needed to force a small business owner to do things he or she should do anyway?

_____

_____

5. Why is it a good idea to review business plans of similar businesses?

_____

_____

Make Academic Connections

6. **Communication** Search for information about how small businesses can make contributions to the economy and prepare a presentation on the topic.

7. **Psychology** Make a list of the characteristics that successful small business owners need. Beside each one, write an "H" if you think that you already have that characteristic. Give an example showing how you have demonstrated that characteristic. Write an "N" if you think that you do not have the characteristic but need it. Then write a one-page plan for how you might develop the characteristics you marked "N."

8. **Government** Locate the SBA office nearest you. Contact this office to ask about the services it provides for small businesses, including how it assists a small business owner in developing a business plan. Write a list of services that are available.

JUMP START

As the Triad Bakery grows, Brianna, Brittney, and Emilio realize that operations are becoming more complex. They have learned how important it is to use all of their resources effectively. They have more employees to deal with and each employee has unique needs. Even though they have some excellent workers, their leadership skills are tested in many ways. What can Brianna, Brittney, and Emilio do to help their employees be as productive as possible in the work that they do?

GOALS

Describe leadership traits and actions

Explain five human relations activities that are important in business

KEY TERMS

leadership, p. 67

human relations, p. 69

Leadership in the Workplace

Successful businesses depend on effective leaders to make sure that work gets done correctly, on time, and profitably. Employees who believe that their leaders respect them have more commitment to their jobs and perform their work tasks better. Becoming a good leader involves learning about and adopting leadership traits and developing human relations skills.

What Is Leadership?

Leadership is more than just being friendly with or liked by employees. It takes skill to get people with different backgrounds and personalities to work well together and to perform required tasks. Leadership is the ability to influence individuals, groups, or teams to accomplish important goals. *Business leadership* includes improving profits, the "bottom line" of the business.

Leadership Characteristics

Leadership characteristics can be learned. Twelve traits and actions of effective leaders are listed below. Read the traits and note the actions that go with them. How many of those traits can you see in people you know? Do you know people who like to take control and make difficult decisions? Do you know others who look to other people for direction and ideas? The workplace needs both kinds of people to accomplish tasks and to improve profits.

TEAMWORK

Work in groups to consider which leadership traits are the easiest to develop, which are the most difficult to develop, and why. Discuss how those traits identified as most difficult can be improved.

CHARACTERISTICS OF EFFECTIVE BUSINESS LEADERS

Traits	Actions
Communication	Listens, speaks, and writes effectively
Confidence	Is willing to make decisions and take responsibility
Cooperation	Works well with others, develops group relationships
Courage	Takes responsible risks, makes unpopular decisions
Dependability	Follows through on commitments
Honesty	Is ethical in decisions and treatment of others
Initiative	Has the ambition and motivation to get tasks done
Intelligence	Has knowledge and understanding
Judgment	Makes decisions carefully and objectively
Objectivity	Looks at all sides of an issue before making a decision
Stability	Is not too emotional or unpredictable
Understanding	Respects the feelings and needs of others

NET Bookmark

Leadership style is the manner and approach of providing direction, implementing plans, and motivating people. In 1939, psychologist Kurt Lewin led a group of researchers to identify three different styles of leadership: authoritarian, participative (democratic), and delegative (laissez-faire). Access www.cengage.com/school/business/21biz and click on the link for Chapter 3. Take the quiz to learn which leadership style best describes you. Do the results surprise you? Why or why not? Follow the *leadership styles* link on the home page and read more about the three styles. Which leadership style probably works best in most situations in the business world? Explain.

www.cengage.com/school/business/21biz

Here are some things you can do now to develop your leadership skills.

- Study leadership and take courses that develop leadership traits.

- Help customers, complete work assignments well, and demonstrate dependability and honesty.

- Observe people in leadership positions. Note those who are effective and consider why you believe they are effective.

- Work with someone who can serve as your mentor—an older brother or sister, a teacher or coach, or a supervisor on your job.

- Demonstrate leadership traits whenever possible. Review the results, analyze what you did well, and ask for constructive feedback from others.

CheckPOINT

What two things could you do now to start developing leadership traits?

_____

_____

Importance of Human Relations

Business managers spend more than half their time in **human relations** activities, that is, interacting with people. They work with employees, customers, people from other businesses and organizations, and other managers and officers in their own companies. Human relations skills are a major factor in determining whether or not a manager is successful.

It is important for business managers to be able to get along with a variety of people, including their own bosses. A business manager needs to develop five basic human relations skills: self-understanding, understanding others, communicating, team building, and developing job satisfaction.

Self-Understanding

It is important to be able to meet the expectations of others, and to do that, business leaders must first understand their own strengths and weaknesses. To improve your human relations skills, you need to be aware of how you get along with others, both individually and in groups.

A manager cannot always do exactly what employees prefer or make decisions with which everyone agrees. However, a manager should never be seen as someone who is unpredictable or unfair. Self-understanding gives the manager self-confidence and the ability to handle problems effectively.

Understanding Others

Effective business leaders recognize that people in a business are more alike than they are different. Recognizing similarities helps develop stronger teams. Differences can also improve a business. If everyone thought and acted the same, there would seldom be new ideas or anyone to question a decision in order to improve upon it.

An effective leader knows each employee and his or her skills, abilities, strengths, and weaknesses. The leader does not treat everyone alike, because employees are not all the same. An effective leader tries to involve each employee in a way that will benefit both the business and the employee.

Why should a manager get to know each employee?

©Piotr Marcinski, 2009/ Used under license from Shutterstock.com

COMMUNICATE

Work with a partner to create a role-play that demonstrates one of the forms of communication in an office setting—formal or informal communication, internal or external communication, vertical or horizontal communication. Present the role-play to the class.

Communicating

Communication is very important in business. Managers must have good communication skills. Communication styles can be classified in several ways. Each communication style has its place in different situations.

Formal communication methods have been established and approved by the business. *Informal* communications are common but unofficial ways that information moves in an organization. Informal communications are sometimes called "the grapevine."

Internal communications occur between managers, employees, and work groups. *External* communications occur between those inside the business and outsiders such as customers, suppliers, government, and other businesses.

Vertical communications move up or down between management and employees. *Horizontal* communications move across the organization at the same level—employee to employee or manager to manager.

Oral communications are words spoken on a person-to-person or person-to-group basis. *Written* communications include notes, letters, memos, reports, bulletin board notices, e-mail, and texting.

Team Building

Teamwork is important in business today. Most businesses are organized into groups or teams. The combined skills and abilities of people on a team are greater than that of individuals working alone. For the team to accomplish its tasks, team members must get along and cooperate.

Managers need team-building skills to unite others to work toward a common goal. Managers should be able to identify problems the group is having and help to resolve those problems quickly.

Developing Job Satisfaction

Managers can influence how employees feel about their jobs. To achieve employee satisfaction, managers must pay attention to the needs and concerns of employees. Employees are most satisfied when their jobs allow them to use their skills and abilities and when they are rewarded for their work.

Job dissatisfaction occurs when there are poor working conditions and ineffective communications. Lack of recognition also often results in dissatisfied employees. Managers must give all employees sincere encouragement and support when it is needed.

CheckPOINT

In your own words, name the five human relations skills successful managers possess.

_____

_____

Think Critically

1. Which of the traits of effective business leaders do you think is the most important? least important? Give reasons why.

   _____

   _____

2. Which of the five human relations skills do you think is most important? least important? Why?

   _____

   _____

3. Why is self-understanding important to a manager?

   _____

   _____

   _____

   _____

4. What are the differences between formal and informal communications, internal and external communications, and vertical and horizontal communications?

   _____

   _____

   _____

Make Academic Connections

5. **Communication** Write a brief speech in which you explain why it is important for each member of a team to understand the work that must be done and to do his or her best to accomplish the team's goals. Give your speech to the class.

6. **Business Math** An effective manager will demonstrate his or her abilities in various ways, such as performing basic computations mentally. Compute the following data without using paper and pencil.

   Teamwork production − Teamwork goals = Variance from goals

Unit	Teamwork Production	Teamwork Goals	Variance from Goals
Unit A	450 items	500 items	−50
Unit B	800	1,000	_____
Unit C	650	500	_____
Totals	_____	_____	_____

GOALS

Define human resources management

Understand employee compensation, benefits, and evaluation

KEY TERMS

human resources management, p. 72

compensation, p. 75

benefits, p. 76

 JUMP START

Brittney has the responsibility for human resources management at the Triad Bakery. The three stores now employ a total of 31 workers, including 9 bakers, 20 salespeople, 1 accountant, and 1 office manager. During the busy seasons, they also employ part-time help from the TandeTemp Agency. Brittney also cooperates with the local technical college's Culinary Arts Department and hires some of its students to work part time as bakers' assistants. Brittney is now in the process of reviewing their employee benefits plan. What types of benefits should be included in that plan?

Banana Stock/ Jupiter Images

Manage Human Resources

People are one of the most important economic resources a business has. They are more important than the technology and materials it uses. Employees must be managed well because of their importance to the success of the business. No matter what the size of the business, employees who have contact with the public affect the image and reputation, and ultimately the profits, of the company.

Human resources management involves all aspects of recruiting, hiring, training, compensating, and evaluating employees. It assures that needed employees are available, productive, adequately compensated, and satisfied with their work. If human resources management does its job well, the company will have employees who do their jobs well. This will result in a profitable business. One of the first steps in human resources management is analyzing current staff and the need for additional employees.

HUMAN RESOURCES IN JAPAN

Japan's Labor Law states that workers cannot be discriminated against based on nationality, sex, creed, or social status. However, the law is very vague. Some companies get around the law by placing women and foreign workers in different job categories and then claiming that the differences in pay are based on job category, not sex or nationality.

Think Critically

How do you think Japan's law on discrimination compares with our law on discrimination regarding women and foreign workers and how we enforce it?

Analyze Staff Needs

Hiring decisions must be made carefully. Putting an individual on the payroll and training that person is a costly process for businesses of all sizes. The only reason to hire a new employee is because the person, in performing the job, will contribute to the company's profitability. For that to happen, the employee must be qualified and compensated fairly. Employees may be classified into four categories: full-time, part-time, permanent, and temporary.

The company must decide whether the person hired is to be a permanent or temporary employee. A permanent employee is one to whom the business makes a long-term commitment. The employee is expected to work for the company as long as the business is profitable and the employee's performance is satisfactory. A temporary employee is hired for a specific time or to complete a specific assignment. Temporary employees are usually hired during a business's busy time period or when a special task needs to be done.

Full-time employees generally work 30 hours or more per week. Others are classified as part-time employees and have a shorter work schedule, with fewer hours each day or fewer work days each week. There may be some combinations of the categories. For instance, an employee can be permanent part-time, working only 20 hours per week, or temporary full-time, working 35 hours per week, but only for a limited period of time.

Determine Employee Qualifications

Before hiring someone, an employer must determine the qualifications—including training, knowledge, and skills—needed for the job. These qualifications must be based on an analysis of the tasks involved in the job. Previous experience at similar jobs may also be required.

Analyzing the work performed by employees is an important human resources management function. Large business firms employ specialists in this area called *job analysts*. Job analysts begin by reviewing, on a step-by-step basis, the work being done by current employees. They determine the skills and knowledge needed to perform the required tasks. Based on that analysis, the analyst develops a *job description*, a written statement that details the qualifications needed and the duties performed on a job.

When new jobs are created or new technology changes job requirements, the job analysis is reviewed and revised. A careful study of the new work tasks to be performed and the requirements of employees needed for new positions is a continuing function of human resources management.

Find New Employees

When job descriptions are completed and up to date, prospective employees who meet the needed skill, knowledge, and experience requirements must be located. This process can be time-consuming and costly. Some businesses use employment agencies that screen candidates before they are referred to the business. The costs of this service may be paid by the employee or the business. The following are common sources of job applicants.

Have you ever responded to a Help Wanted sign?

- Career placement offices at schools, colleges, and universities
- Referrals by current and former employees
- Public and private employment agencies
- Newspaper classified advertising
- Internet career services
- Job and career fairs
- Company websites
- Radio and television advertising
- Help wanted signs
- Industry publications
- The company's employment office

Most companies ask prospective employees to fill out an employment application. The answers provide personal information on the applicant's education, as well as work experience history. The application may also ask about specific skills related to the jobs and names of people who can serve as references. It is important to fill out employment applications completely and honestly.

Small businesses may hire young people and give them their first work experience. Performing well on your first job is an important factor in developing a good work history. When selecting new employees, a business will usually check with a former employer to find out about work habits, attendance records, length of employment, and the person's ability to work well with others as a member of a team. Selecting the right employee for the right job is the ultimate goal of human resources management.

CheckPOINT

Define human resources management in your own words.

_____

_____

Compensation, Benefits, and Evaluation

Why do people work? The main reason, of course, is to earn an income so they can support themselves, a parent, and/or a family. Other reasons may include the desire to make a contribution to the economy, to use the knowledge and skills they have developed, and to identify with a profession or business. Compensating people fairly and adequately for the work they perform is one of the important human resources management tasks. **Compensation** is the amount of money paid to an employee for work performed. Compensation is made up of two parts—salary and wages and benefits.

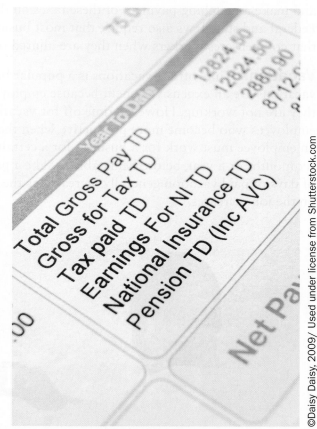

How does a salary differ from wages?

©Daisy Daisy, 2009/ Used under license from Shutterstock.com

Salary and Wages

Salary and wages are direct payments to employees for work completed. A *salary* is a fixed amount of money paid to an employee regardless of the number of hours worked. A salary is usually stated on an annual basis; for example, $35,000 a year. *Wages* are payments for labor made on an hourly, daily, or per-unit basis; for example, $8 per hour.

TEAMWORK

Form a team. List and discuss the different kinds of employee benefits. Consider the importance of each one and decide which two of the benefits would be most desired. Compare the results of each team. Which of the benefits were most often selected as the two most desired?

Benefits

Benefits include compensation in forms other than a direct payment to the employee. Examples of benefits are insurance, vacations, retirement plans, onsite childcare, and health and fitness programs. Benefits, sometimes called *fringe benefits*, are a costly addition to the expense of employee compensation. For all businesses, this cost is equal to an additional 20 to 40 percent of an employee's wages or salary. For an employee who earns $8 per hour, that employee's cost to the business is between $9.60 (20%) and $11.20 (40%) per hour. If a company has a total payroll of $300,000, fringe benefits would add $60,000 to $120,000 to their operating cost. For the employee, an advantage of some benefits is that the extra amount of compensation is not added to the wage or salary and the employee does not have to pay taxes on that amount.

Some benefits are negotiated by unions or employee groups. Other benefits are required by state and federal law. For example, most businesses must pay hourly employees extra for overtime hours worked. Businesses are also required by law to withhold social security and Medicare taxes from employees' wages and make a matching payment of these taxes on their employee's behalf. Federal and state laws also require that most businesses pay money into a fund that compensates workers when they are injured or unemployed.

Vacations Time off for vacations is a popular benefit for employees. Paid vacations are an expensive benefit because employees are paid wages when they are not working. However, time off for vacations may result in satisfied employees who become more productive when they return to work. Usually, an employee must work for a business for a certain period of time, perhaps six months or a year, before being able to take a paid vacation. The number of days of paid vacation generally increases as the employee's number of years on the job increases.

©Elena Elisseeva, 2009/ Used under license from Shutterstock.com

Vacations are a common benefit offered by employers. What other employee benefits would be important to you?

Insurance Some employees may be offered insurance plans, including health, life, dental, and disability insurance. Because of the rapidly rising costs of health insurance, employees may be required to pay part of their coverage.

Other Benefits Other benefits include retirement plans, sick leave, personal days, and flexible work schedules. Costs of benefit programs are high and continue to increase, and as a result, some businesses offer *cafeteria plans*. This means a certain amount of money is allocated to each employee for his or her benefits. The employee selects the preferred benefits. If the costs of the benefits selected are less than the money allocated, the employee can receive the difference in extra pay. If costs are higher, the employee pays the difference.

Evaluation

Managers evaluate the work of employees on a regular basis. Developing evaluation procedures and forms is the responsibility of the human resources department. Managers are trained to be objective in completing evaluations and in holding evaluation conferences with employees. The results of evaluations are kept in the employee's personnel file. Evaluations work hand in hand with compensation. Pay raises are often the result of evaluations. The amount of the raise may be directly tied to the evaluation "score."

Evaluation Process Performance evaluations focus on the specific job duties of each employee. There is a review of the important work traits expected of all employees. Included are factors such as communication, interpersonal relationships, quality and quantity of work, and ethical behavior.

Evaluation decisions are based on observations of the employee's performance and on an evaluation of the quality of work produced. Managers use an evaluation form to identify each employee's strengths and areas that need improvement.

Evaluation Conference After the manager completes the evaluation form, a formal meeting is held with the employee. The purpose of this conference is to discuss the results of the evaluation and to plan for any needed improvement. This conference can be uncomfortable for both the manager and the employee, but its purpose is to benefit both the employee and the company and should be meaningful and positive. The end result should be a reasonable agreement on the employee's performance, goals, and plans for the future. It should also identify the support that the manager and the company will give the employee to help him or her improve performance.

CheckPOINT

What is the connection between compensation and evaluations?

_____

_____

Think Critically

1. Should a business hire someone just because the person wants or needs a job? Why or why not?

2. Why is a job description important to both employees and managers?

3. Would you prefer to have a higher wage without fringe benefits or a lower wage with fringe benefits? Explain your answer.

4. What should be the end result of the evaluation conference, and why is that important to the employee?

Make Academic Connections

5. **Government** Human resources managers must work with the Occupational Safety and Health Administration (OSHA). Research OSHA to find out what its purpose is and how it works with businesses to try to improve the workplace. Then write a one-page summary of your findings.

6. **Careers** Job titles in the human resources management area include human resources director, recruiter, job analyst, and compensation specialist. Using the Occupational Outlook Handbook, the Internet, or other resources, read about human resources management job titles that you locate. Select several and write one paragraph about each one explaining what you have learned and what interests you about them.

7. **Communication** Read some help wanted ads in newspapers, magazines, the Internet, or other sources. Select two or more ads that list benefits. Would these benefits attract you to these employers more than others who do not list their benefits? Why or why not?

JUMP START

Brianna is good at working with figures and likes to keep records. She handles the financial management for the Triad Bakery. When they first started the business, she determined how much money it would take to buy the basic things they needed to begin operations. Now that the business is operating soundly, she keeps records of income from sales, and expenditures for supplies, materials, wages, taxes, insurance, and other items. Brianna and Chen, the company accountant, use computer technology and software to prepare budgets, income statements, and balance sheets. How often should each of these financial records be prepared?

GOALS

Explain how budgeting relates to financial planning

Describe two kinds of financial reports prepared by businesses

KEY TERMS

business budget, p. 80

financial record, p. 82

income statement, p. 82

balance sheet, p. 83

Financial Management

One of the reasons why small businesses often fail is that they do not manage their finances properly. Money management is a serious issue for all businesses regardless of size. You have learned that a financial plan is an important part of a business plan. Businesses must wisely manage the money they take in and pay out to become profitable and to stay in business.

Financial Planning

Profit is what is left over after the business pays all of its expenses. It takes most businesses a year or two before they begin earning a profit. It is important for business owners and managers to know what their financial position is and where they are heading financially.

Why is it important for a business to estimate its expenses?

One financial planning document is called a business budget. A **business budget** is a detailed plan for meeting the financial needs of the business. It has two main purposes: (1) anticipating sources and amounts of income, and (2) predicting the types and amounts of expenses for a specific business activity or for the entire business.

The money that a business receives is called *income*, or *revenue*. Most of a business's revenue comes from sales of its products or services. The way in which the revenue comes in is important. Most businesses rely on credit, and therefore, many sales are not paid for until 30 days or longer after the sale. Financial managers use a *statement of cash flow* to show the actual cash a business receives and has available on a daily basis.

Businesses cannot operate without spending money. The operating costs of a business are referred to as *expenses*. Expenses can include employee wages and benefits, advertising, rent, utilities, and supplies.

The business must be able to identify and predict the amount of each source of income and each type of expense. Budgeting is an important part of that process. The budget process requires an understanding of financial information, computer skills, basic math abilities, and effective communication skills. Basic steps to follow in creating and effectively using a budget are

- Determining the type of revenue and expenses to be included
- Gathering information from business records and other sources
- Creating the budget using available technology
- Distributing and discussing the budget with those who will use the information for decision making

Types of Budgets

Budgets provide detailed plans for the financial needs of individuals, families, and businesses. A business budget projects the amounts of income and expenses.

TEAMWORK

Form teams representing consulting companies. Assume there is a request to help develop a start-up budget for an individual who wants to open a computer repair service business. The capital needed is $150,000. Your team must decide what to include in a start-up budget. Use your own assumptions to come up with a start-up budget for this business.

Budgeting is an important step in financial planning. A well-prepared budget helps a business avoid costly financial mistakes. A budget lets managers know how the business is doing in terms of meeting its financial goals. Three types of business budgets are the start-up budget, operating budget, and cash budget.

Start-Up Budget The *start-up budget* is used to plan income and expenses from the beginning of a new business or a major business expansion until it becomes profitable. Buildings and equipment must be purchased. Most start-ups require very large expenditures of capital to begin. Materials, supplies, new employees, licenses, and advertising are examples of what are needed before a company can begin to sell its product or service. The start-up needs for new businesses can cost hundreds of thousands of dollars.

Money to pay for start-up costs comes from many sources. Obtaining capital through loans from a financial institution is common. Before lending any money, a lending institution will want to see a budget and business plan.

Operating Budget The financial plan for the day-to-day operations of the business is called the *operating budget*. It covers a specific period of time: three months, six months, or a full year. This budget follows this equation:

$$\text{Revenue} - \text{Expenses} = \text{Profit (or Loss)}$$

All anticipated revenues and expenses are listed, and the planned net profit or loss is shown.

Cash Budget The *cash budget* is an estimate of the money expected to be received and paid out over a specific period of time. It lets the manager know if there is a period when cash must be borrowed to meet expenses. Even profitable businesses may have times when adequate cash is not available because of high expenses or a delay in receiving payments from customers. Nevertheless, money must always be on hand to pay expenses.

Business Math Connection

Calculate the net profit or loss for the month for Galaxy Comic Books where cash sales were $3,560, charge sales were $1,240, and other revenue was $165. Salaries were $2,450, advertising was $200, rent was $550, and supplies were $120.

SOLUTION
The formula for calculating net profit or loss is

Revenue	−	Expenses	= Profit (or Loss)
$(3,560 + 1,240 + 165)$	−	$(2,450 + 200 + 550 + 120)$	= Profit (or Loss)
4,965	−	3,320	= 1,645

The net profit was $1,645.

Financial Records

Budgets are the financial plans, or forecasts, for a business. To find out if the plans have been achieved, the business needs financial records. A **financial record** shows the financial performance of a business. The following records are commonly maintained to document the performance of a business.

- Asset records name the buildings and equipment owned by the business, their original and current value, and the amount owed if money was borrowed to purchase the assets.

- Depreciation records identify the amount that assets have decreased in value due to their age and usage.

- Inventory records identify the type and number of products on hand for sale.

- Payroll records contain information on all employees' compensation and benefits.

- Cash records list all cash received and spent by the business.

- Records of accounts identify purchases made using credit. An accounts payable record shows credit purchases made by the company, including the amount purchased, paid, and owed. An accounts receivable record identifies credit purchases by customers and the status of each account.

- Tax records show all taxes collected, owed, and paid. There are many payroll and other taxes that a business must pay, including taxes withheld from employees' paychecks and, in some cases, sales taxes.

Financial records are used to prepare two important financial statements: the income statement and the balance sheet. These statements are important not only to the managers of the business but also to investors and lenders.

The Income Statement

An **income statement** is a financial statement that shows revenues, expenses, and net income (profit) or loss for a period of time. The income statement usually covers a period of six months or a year but may cover shorter periods, such as a month, in a new business. The income statement prepared at the end of the year is important because it shows how the business did for the entire year. It is the basis for the payment of taxes and decision making.

The income statement for the Overland Design Company illustrates some of the categories of revenue and expenses that are shown in a typical statement. Also, an income statement often has accompanying notes that explain items in the statement. For instance, if charge sales in a period are substantially greater than they were in previous periods, the notes will explain why.

Overland Design Company Income Statement For the Year Ended December 31, 20—		
Revenue		
Cash sales	$ 38,200	
Charge sales	180,600	
Other revenue	12,900	
Total Revenue		$231,700
Expenses		
Salaries and wages	$ 70,800	
Marketing	22,250	
Administrative costs	31,900	
Materials and supplies	24,800	
Other expenses	19,100	
Total Expenses		168,850
Net Income		$ 62,850

The Balance Sheet

A **balance sheet** is a financial statement that lists a business's assets (what a company owns) and liabilities (what a company owes). It also shows the owner's equity, which is the value of the owner's investment in the business (sometimes called net worth). The equation for owner's equity is

$$\text{Assets} - \text{Liabilities} = \text{Owner's Equity}$$

In a balance sheet, the two sides of the statement must be in balance. As shown in the balance sheet for Schreiber Automotives, Inc., below, the right-hand side adds the total of the liabilities and the owner's equity to show that they equal the value of the assets on the left-hand side. The basic equation for the balance sheet is

$$\text{Assets} = \text{Liabilities} + \text{Owner's Equity}$$

Schreiber Automotives, Inc. Balance Sheet December 31, 20—			
Assets		**Liabilities**	
Cash	$35,850	Accounts payable	$103,300
Investments	40,000	Payroll taxes	22,000
Accounts receivable	42,375	Mortgage	126,800
Buildings	250,000	**Total Liabilities**	$252,100
Equipment	120,000		
		Owner's Equity	$236,125
		Total Liabilities and	
Total Assets	**$488,225**	**Owner's Equity**	**$488,225**

The balance sheet does not give a picture of the business over a period of time. Instead it shows what the business is worth on a particular date, usually the end of a year. One of the uses of the balance sheet is to compare the owner's equity of the business with previous years. If the business is doing well, the owner's equity will tend to increase from year to year. Some businesses include comparative data from previous years in their balance sheets.

Both the income statement and the balance sheet are important financial reports. Business managers review these reports and discuss them to determine how the business is performing. Comparisons of the company's operations, as well as comparisons with similar businesses, are made from period to period. Improving the profitability of the company is the primary objective when managing financial resources.

Maintaining Financial Records

Keeping financial records and statements accurate and up to date is not the problem today that it was in the past. Preparing and maintaining financial documents used to be an expensive and time-consuming process. Often done manually using paper documents, it took special care to complete, save, and protect the records.

Technology today is changing the way financial information is collected. Much information is now collected using point-of-production and point-of-sale technology, such as scanners, touch screens, and personal digital assistants (PDA's). Data files are transferred from the places where information is collected and sent to the computers of the people who prepare the financial records.

How has technology changed the way financial records are prepared and maintained?

Technology is also changing the way financial records are prepared and maintained. Businesses use computerized financial systems that have templates for each financial record. The software completes the necessary mathematical calculations, updates records, and makes comparisons of those records with budgets. The software can even complete what-if comparisons to help managers determine the impact of changes in budgets and financial performance.

CheckPOINT

Name several kinds of financial records commonly kept by businesses.

_____

_____

Think Critically

1. Why is a business budget an important tool in managing financial resources?

_____

_____

2. Why do businesses need a cash budget and an operating budget?

_____

_____

_____

3. You are interested in becoming a partner in a business that has been operating for the past five years. Which of the financial statements would be the most important for you to see? Why?

_____

_____

4. Why would a business manager want to compare the company's financial statements with those of similar companies?

_____

_____

Make Academic Connections

5. **Consumer Economics** Locate magazine articles that discuss personal and family budgeting. Write a paragraph about the similarities and differences between a family's and a business's operating budget.

6. **Accounting** The balance sheet for Schreiber Automotives, Inc., contains titles of five kinds of assets and three kinds of liabilities. Find an accounting textbook or a company's annual report online. Look up other common types of assets and liabilities and compile a list.

7. **Business Math** Revenue and expense figures for Lisa's Boutique for the past three months are as follows. Create a spreadsheet to compute the net income or loss for each month.

Month 1: Cash sales, $7,890; charge sales, $11,300; other revenue, $250; salaries, $9,600; advertising, $1,500; rent, $1,800; supplies, $500

Month 2: Cash sales, $8,820; charge sales, $12,360; other revenue, $450; salaries, $10,120; advertising, $2,500; rent, $1,800; supplies, $350

Month 3: Cash sales, $9,540; charge sales, $2,450; other revenue, $300; salaries, $9,840; advertising, $2,500; rent, $1,800; supplies, $900

Chapter Summary

3.1	**Small Business Management**	**A.** Successful small business owners are independent, persistent, self-motivated, and hard working. **B.** The key elements of a business plan include a description of the business and the competition, a marketing plan, a customer analysis, an operation plan, and a financial plan.
3.2	**Business Leadership**	**A.** Effective leaders get people to work together and to perform required tasks. **B.** There are five basic human relations skills important to managing people: self-understanding, understanding others, communicating, team building, and developing job satisfaction.
3.3	**Human Resources Management**	**A.** Human resources management deals with recruiting, hiring, training, compensating, and evaluating employees. **B.** Handling employee compensation and giving performance evaluations are important human resources management tasks.
3.4	**Financial Resources Management**	**A.** Business budgets help businesses meet financial needs and goals. Types of budgets include start-up budgets, operating budgets, and cash budgets. **B.** Financial records are important in reporting the financial status and progress of a company. The income statement and the balance sheet are two important financial statements.

Vocabulary Builder

Choose the term that best fits the definition. Write the letter of the answer in the space provided. Some terms may not be used.

_____ 1. Financial statement showing revenues, expenses, and net income/loss

_____ 2. Recruiting, hiring, training, compensating, and evaluating employees

_____ 3. Government agency that provides services to small businesses

_____ 4. The amount of money paid to employees for work performed

_____ 5. A record of the financial performance of a business

_____ 6. Financial statement that lists a business's assets and liabilities

_____ 7. Written description of a business idea and how it will be carried out

_____ 8. Detailed plan for meeting the financial needs of the business

_____ 9. Compensation other than a direct payment to the employee

_____ 10. An independent business with fewer than 500 employees

a. balance sheet

b. benefits

c. business budget

d. business plan

e. compensation

f. financial record

g. human relations

h. human resources management

i. income statement

j. leadership

k. small business

l. Small Business Administration (SBA)

Review Concepts

Point Your Browser

www.cengage.com/
school/business/21biz

11. What are five characteristics of successful small business owners?

_____

_____

_____

12. What are sources of new ideas for a business?

_____

_____

_____

13. Describe two key features of a business plan.

_____

_____

_____

_____

14. What are the twelve traits of effective business leaders?

_____

_____

_____

15. What are eight communication styles found in businesses?

_____

_____

_____

16. What is human resources management?

_____

_____

_____

_____

17. What is a job description?

_____

_____

_____

_____

18. What are the two parts of employee compensation? Define each.

_____

_____

_____

_____

_____

19. Name the two purposes of the evaluation conference.

_____

_____

_____

20. Why is it important for businesses to keep financial records?

_____

_____

_____

21. Describe an income statement and a balance sheet.

_____

_____

_____

_____

Apply What You Learned

22. How can working a part-time or full-time job now be helpful in starting your own business later?

_____

_____

_____

23. Why do you think there is an emphasis in the workplace today on employees being good team members?

_____

_____

_____

24. If you were to give references on a job application, who are three people you would list? What do you think each person could say about you that would help you get the job?

_____

_____

_____

_____

25. Consider a job you would like to have someday. Write a job description of that job, describing the job qualifications and duties.

_____

_____

_____

_____

Make Academic Connections

26. **Social Studies** Over the past several years, the Small Business Administration has sponsored special programs and published special materials to help women and minorities succeed in small business. Use the library or Internet to learn more about these programs and materials. Write a paragraph about SBA programs for women and minorities.

27. **Communication** Teamwork is becoming more and more important in the workplace. You are a training director and will be addressing a group of new employees. Write a brief outline of major points you will make about why teamwork is important and what would be expected of the new employees. Give your presentation in class.

28. **Government** The Service Corps of Retired Executives (SCORE) is an important group sponsored by the SBA. Using the Internet and other sources, find out about some specific ways that SCORE helps small business owners. Write a paragraph summarizing your findings.

29. **Accounting** Compute the owner's equity for each company, and then answer the questions that follow.

Assets − Liabilities = Owner's Equity

COMPANY OWNER'S EQUITY COMPARISON			
Company	Assets	Liabilities	Owner's Equity
Gerig	$ 15,800	$ 9,600	_____
Haugen	29,315	27,100	_____
Holihan	135,985	112,960	_____
Loether	197,810	190,790	_____
Nees	27,800	10,100	_____
Sowls	46,500	28,900	_____

Which company has the largest owner's equity? _____

Which company has the lowest owner's equity? _____

What is the amount of the difference between the highest and the lowest owner's equity? _____

Ethical Dilemma

30. You are a human resources manager interviewing a job applicant for an opening in the accounting department. The job will require the employee to work overtime during busy seasons, such as tax season. When you learn that the candidate has children, you become concerned that she will not be able to commit to working longer hours when needed. You decide not to hire her. Is this fair? Explain your answer.

CHAPTER 4

The Global Economy

4.1 International Business

4.2 Government in the U.S. Economy

4.3 Business Ethics and Social Responsibility

Careers in Business

NIKE, INC.

Nike, Inc., based in Beaverton, Oregon, designs and sells footwear, apparel, equipment, and accessories for athletes. Nike operates in more than 160 countries. The company's 30,000+ employees are located on six continents. Nike products are sold globally as well, earning total annual revenues of $19.2 billion for the company in a recent year.

Trade finance coordinators at Nike prepare letters of credit, the documents used to pay foreign producers. They also work with banks and suppliers to ensure that the international transactions are completed properly.

Nike's trade finance coordinators need to understand international finance and accounting. Applicants for the position should have two years of international banking or finance experience. They also must have good decision-making skills and the ability to communicate cross-culturally.

Think Critically

1. Is working in the world of international finance of interest to you? Why or why not?

2. Why is the ability to communicate cross-culturally important for trade finance coordinators at Nike?

PROJECT | Global Business and You

Photodisc/Getty Images

Project Objectives

- Consider the advantages and disadvantages of international trade
- Consider the impact of government on international trade policies
- Relate ethics and social responsibility to the practice of international trade

Getting Started

Read the Project Process below. Make a list of any materials you need.

- Make an inventory of imported goods and products you have in your household. Include sporting goods, appliances, and electronic devices in your inventory. Countries of origin generally are identified on tags or labels Use the following headings:

GOODS MADE IN OTHER COUNTRIES

Item   Country of Origin

- Consolidate the individual inventories into one inventory for the class.

Project Process

4.1 Discuss the impact of U.S. international trade policies on the goods listed in the consolidated inventory. Make a list of issues mentioned.

4.2 What impact would the governmental issues in Lesson 4.2 have on the goods listed in your inventory?

4.3 Discuss how ethics and social responsibility might relate to doing business globally. Make a list of issues mentioned.

Chapter Review

Project Wrap-up   Hold a class debate on the following issue: "The U.S. economy would be better if goods and services were not imported from other countries." As a class, evaluate this statement and come to a consensus.

©Anyka, 2009/ Used under license from Shutterstock.com

GOALS

Explain the difference between imports and exports

Describe three barriers to international trade

KEY TERMS

international business, p. 92

imports, p. 93

exports, p. 93

balance of trade, p. 93

quota, p. 95

tariff, p. 95

embargo, p. 96

 JUMP START

Brianna, Brittney, and Emilio are again looking for ways to expand the Triad Bakery. They now have 12 locations in 5 U.S. cities. They are considering expanding into Canada because they already have one location 20 miles from the Canadian border that is very successful. They are also considering exporting their products into the European market. What issues will the partners need to consider so that they can properly conduct business in Canada and in Europe?

Trade with Other Nations

Doing business in a global marketplace presents challenges for all countries. A business must factor in how currency exchanges, trade barriers, and the different laws and business practices of other countries will affect them. Although most of a country's economic activities take place within its borders, trade with other countries can be an essential component for success.

The United States is one of the leaders in international business. **International business** refers to business activities necessary for creating, shipping, and selling goods and services across national borders. International business is frequently referred to as *foreign* or *world trade*.

Our nation has many natural resources, a skilled work force, and modern technologies. However, we cannot provide all the goods consumers want so it is necessary to do business with companies throughout the world. We have many imports and exports. For example, coffee comes to us from Brazil, crude oil from Saudi Arabia, and wool from Australia. Farm machinery, medicines, and office equipment that we produce are in demand throughout the world.

Imports

Goods and services that U.S. companies buy from other countries are called **imports**. Imports to the United States account for the total supply of our bananas, coffee, cocoa, spices, tea, silk, and crude rubber. About half of all crude oil and fish comes from imports. Imports account for a large amount of the supply of carpets, sugar, and leather gloves. The United States also imports mica, tin, zinc, industrial diamonds, and several other metals.

Without international trade, many of the products that consumers buy would not be available or might cost more. Some countries can sell goods at lower prices because their labor costs are much lower. In some cases, consumers perceive imports to be of higher quality than the same item made in the United States. Or consumers may just prefer products from other countries, such as Norwegian sweaters, French perfumes, and Swiss watches.

Exports

The goods and services that U.S. companies sell to other countries are called **exports**. U.S. exports benefit consumers in other economies just as imports to the United States benefit you as a consumer. U.S. exports that are popular in other countries include farm machinery, medicines, food, books, movies, TV programs, and plastics.

Producing goods and services for export is good for the U.S. workforce too. About one out of every six jobs in the United States depends on international business for its existence. Jobs that are supported by international trade also tend to pay high wages. The U.S. Exports and Imports table shows the value of exported and imported goods between the United States and seven countries in a recent year.

A country's **balance of trade** is the difference between its exports and its imports. When exports are greater than imports, a *positive* balance of trade occurs. When imports are greater than exports, a *negative* balance of trade occurs.

U.S. EXPORTS AND IMPORTS
(in billions of dollars)

Country	Exports	Imports
Canada	$261	$339
Japan	65	139
Mexico	151	216
European Union	272	368
Netherlands	40	21
Taiwan	25	36
China	70	338

International Currency

One of the challenges faced by businesses that export and import is the variety of currencies in the world. Each nation has its own banking system and its own kind of money. For instance, Russia uses the ruble, Venezuela the bolivar, the European Union the euro, and the Netherlands the guilder.

When U.S. companies trade with companies in other countries, currency must be exchanged. Most large banks provide currency exchange services for businesses. The *exchange rate* is the value of a currency of one country compared with the currency of another country. When our U.S. currency is

Business Math Connection

Calculate the balance of trade for two countries. Country A has exports of $825 billion and imports of $610 billion. Country B has exports of $500 billion and imports of $895 billion. Determine whether the balance of trade in each country is positive or negative.

SOLUTION

The formula for calculating balance of trade is

$$\text{Balance of trade} = \text{Exports} - \text{Imports}$$

$$\text{Country A: Balance of trade} = \$825 \text{ billion} - \$610 \text{ billion}$$
$$= \$215 \text{ billion}$$

$$\text{Country B: Balance of trade} = \$500 \text{ billion} - \$895 \text{ billion}$$
$$= -\$395 \text{ billion}$$

Country A has a positive balance of trade, and Country B has a negative balance of trade.

valued lower than the currency of the country we are trading with, prices for our goods in the other country will be lower. When the value of currency in the other country is lower, our goods will sell for a higher price in that country. Exchange rates fluctuate constantly. Recent examples are shown in the exchange rate table.

EXAMPLES OF EXCHANGE RATES			
Country	Currency	Units per USD*	Value in USD
Australia	dollar	1.1606	0.8615
Canada	dollar	1.0792	0.9265
China	renminbi	6.8382	0.1462
Egypt	pound	5.5628	0.1797
European Union	euro	0.6887	1.4519
Japan	yen	92.2618	0.0108
Mexico	new peso	13.4756	0.0742
New Zealand	dollar	1.4360	0.6963
Russia	ruble	31.1174	0.0321
South Africa	rand	7.5429	0.1325
South Korea	won	1,225.7900	0.0008
Taiwan	dollar	32.7430	0.0305
United Kingdom	pound	0.6043	1.6547
Venezuela	bolivar	2.1500	0.4651

*USD = United States Dollar

DID YOU KNOW ?

The United States conducts trade with more than 240 countries.

What is the difference between an import and an export?

_____

_____

Barriers to International Trade

Governments can establish laws and policies that affect international business. These laws and policies are barriers to international trade designed to control imports, exports, and sales of goods and services for the benefit of their economies. Three common barriers are quotas, tariffs, and embargoes. The culture, traditions, and religion of a country can also create informal trade barriers.

Quotas

One device governments use to regulate international trade sets a limit on the quantity of a product that can be imported or exported. This quantity limit is referred to as a **quota**.

Countries that export oil, for example, might put quotas on crude oil that will be sent to other countries. This ensures that the supply will remain low and prices will stay at a certain level or increase. Sometimes quotas are placed on a country's imports to express disapproval of a specific policy or social behavior. Another common use of quotas is to shield a country's "infant industries," which need protection from competition to give them a chance to develop into successful, competitive businesses. Our government has imposed quotas in the past on sugar, cattle, dairy products, and textiles.

Tariffs

Another device governments use to regulate international trade is the tariff. A **tariff** is a tax a government places on certain imported products to cause the price of those products to increase in the country's markets. For instance, an imported bicycle might normally sell for $240. If there is a tariff of 20 percent on that import, it would have to sell for 20 percent more, or $288.

$240 × 0.20 = $48 tariff
$240 + $48 = $288 selling price

Why would the U.S. government place a quota on certain imports, such as sugar?

©Aptyp_koK, 2009/ Used under license from Shutterstock.com

Tech Literacy

LANGUAGE TRANSLATORS

There are times when you might receive a phone call from a business colleague who speaks a language different from yours. Today's technology solves the problem of translation with computerized translators that recognize speech in one language and convert the spoken words into another language. Three components work together, resulting in a voice synthesizer that speaks the translated version. Some translators can handle as many as 34 languages. Handheld translators are also available for business travelers.

THINK CRITICALLY

What do you see as advantages and disadvantages of using computerized language translators as a part of international business?

The higher price on an imported bicycle might cause buyers to select a bicycle made in their own country.

Some tariffs are a set amount per pound, gallon, or other unit. Others are computed on the value of the good, as in the example of the bicycle. Higher tariffs lead to decreased demand for the imported product and, therefore, fewer imports and competition for a country's own products. Some individuals in the United States believe that the government should use tariffs more often to protect jobs from foreign competition.

Embargoes

If governments wish to do so, they can stop the import or export of goods and services completely. This action against another country is called an **embargo**. There are many reasons for imposing an embargo. Governments may wish to protect their own businesses from international competition more than either the quota or the tariff will achieve. A government sometimes imposes embargoes to express disapproval of the actions or policies of another country.

Embargoes are used sparingly. They can create a backlash from the countries involved and often do not correct the problem at hand.

TEAMWORK

Break into two groups to debate the pros and cons of using trade barriers, such as quotas, tariffs, and embargoes. Discuss the negative and positive impacts of these barriers on the U.S. economy and the U.S. consumers in the marketplace.

CheckPOINT

State the difference between a tariff, a quota, and an embargo.

_____

_____

_____

Think Critically

1. Do you think companies in the United States should do business with companies in other countries? Why or why not?

_____

_____

_____

2. Why do you think there are so many currencies in the world? Would it be better to have just one currency? Explain your answer.

_____

_____

_____

_____

3. What could be done to make U.S. products more competitive in other nations?

_____

_____

_____

4. On what basis can setting tariffs be justified? Who benefits from tariffs? Who does not benefit?

_____

_____

_____

_____

Make Academic Connections

5. **Languages** The language of international business is English. Yet it is desirable for people in the United States to be familiar with other languages. Look up some common expressions (such as "good morning," "how are you?" and "thank you") in Spanish, German, and French. Find a reference that tells how to pronounce the words. Write the expressions on a sheet of paper. Practice speaking those phrases with your classmates.

6. **Business Math** For each of the seven countries shown in the U.S. Exports and Imports table on page 93, compute the U.S. balance of trade with that country. Indicate whether the balance of trade with each country is positive or negative. What does this indicate about the U.S. economy?

JUMP START

The success of the Triad Bakery has led to competing bakeries copying the look and taste of its products. The partners have recently learned that other bakeries have been specifically advertising and promoting their versions of "Triple T cookies," which is the name of one of Triad Bakery's most popular cookies containing unique ingredients and a special design. Brittney is currently working toward her MBA degree. In one of her business classes, she learned that the government has methods of protecting the intangible property of individuals and businesses, such as the Triple T cookie name. What specific type of government protection would defend the Triad Bakery against competitors offering their Triple T cookies?

©Mike Neale, 2009/ Used under license from Shutterstock.com

Government as a Protector

Governments are known to play an important role in a country's economic system. You have learned that citizens who perform their economic roles influence decisions made by governments. Governments enact laws that protect individuals and businesses in the marketplace. They also perform some of the activities of a business.

Laws are enacted and regulations established to protect citizens' rights. Services such as police and fire services and the armed forces protect citizens and businesses. Governments enact and enforce safety regulations to protect workers. Governments protect individuals and businesses by enforcing contracts, protecting intellectual property rights, and regulating public utilities.

Enforcing Contracts

An agreement to exchange goods and services for something of value, usually money, is called a **contract**. Contracts are fundamental to doing business, and they may be written or unwritten. To be enforceable, however, contracts must include the following basic elements.

- *Agreement* An offer must be made, and an acceptance must occur.

- *Competent parties* Those entering into the contract must be of legal age and must be mentally competent.

- *Consideration* Something of measurable value must be exchanged by the parties involved.

- *Legality* The contract must be for a product or service that may be legally sold. There must not be any fraud or deception existing in the agreement.

Why should you closely examine a contract before signing it?

©Feng Yu, 2009/ Used under license from Shutterstock.com

Both consumers and businesses benefit from government enforcement of contracts. Written contracts, once signed, bind both parties to what is in the agreement. It is never a good idea to sign a contract without reading the entire document because all parts of that contract are enforceable. Verbal contracts are also valid if they meet all of the enforceable provisions. For example, if you agree to have some equipment repaired, the work must be performed as agreed upon before you pay the amount owed. Disputes over whether or not the work was done correctly and how much you owe will be based on the agreement that was made orally. The matter can be settled in court based on the oral contract.

Cross-Cultural Relationships

WRITING REQUIREMENTS FOR CONTRACTS

The laws regarding writing requirements for contracts differ among nations. The United Nations Convention on Contracts for the International Sale of Goods (CISG) was in effect in 71 countries in 2008, including the United States. Under the CISG, contracts for the sale of goods among nations need not be in writing (Article 11). The CISG is said to be one of the most successful international uniform laws and is having a great influence on "worldwide trans-border commerce."

Think Critically

What are the advantages and disadvantages of putting any contract in writing? Of putting international contracts in writing?

Protecting Intellectual Property Rights

Intellectual property is purely intangible, with no physical characteristics—a person cannot touch it. Intellectual property includes patents, copyrights, and trademarks.

When individuals create new products, they may obtain a patent. A *patent* gives the inventor of the product the exclusive right to make, use, or sell that item for a period of 20 years. Without this protection, inventors of new products would have no ownership rights. The patent itself can be sold or marketed by its owner.

Copyrights protect the creative work of authors, artists, and composers. Copyright protection continues for the life of the person receiving the copyright and extends 70 years beyond that. Copyrights are identified with the symbol ©.

Another form of protection given to a business by a government is a trademark. A *trademark* is a word, letter, or symbol associated with a specific company or product. Many goods are sold largely based on the trademark, sometimes called a logo. The Nike brand name and "swoosh" symbol are examples of trademarks. A trademark can become very valuable.

Why does intellectual property need protection?

©Mariday, 2009/ Used under license from Shutterstock.com

When conducting business globally, intellectual property rights are a concern. Although intellectual property rights are protected by several international agreements, violations are common in other countries, such as China. Violations can include counterfeit products or *piracy*, which is the illegal use of intellectual property. Counterfeiting results in financial losses for the originator of the product. The U.S. government must continue to work with international agencies to strengthen the enforcement of intellectual property laws.

Regulating Public Utilities

A *public utility* is an organization that supplies a good or service that all citizens need and use. These needs include local telephone service, water, gas, and electricity. Governments regulate public utilities by giving them exclusive rights to operate in a given market or community. This helps to avoid expensive duplication of items such as telephone poles and power lines. Such duplication would make the business inefficient and more costly to consumers.

Some utility companies are privately owned. Traditionally, however, they have been closely regulated by the government for the good of consumers. Regulations govern rates and quality standards. The recent trend toward deregulation of such services is said by some to allow competition to benefit consumers.

CheckPOINT

Give three examples of how the government acts as a protector.

_____

_____

_____

Government as a Business

Governments provide a number of goods and services to citizens and businesses. Examples are police forces, fire stations, court systems, parks, libraries, schools, and streets. To provide these services, governments must conduct some of the activities of a business. They must buy goods and services, employ workers, raise revenue, and borrow money.

Buying Goods and Services

Governments spend a lot of money buying products and services. Among these purchases are police cars, road-building materials, and telephone services. Data gathered and purchased by various government agencies are used by different organizations for planning and decision making.

In its role as a business, governments are a major economic force. Many businesses depend on government contracts for their survival. Some construction companies keep their workforces employed through the construction of roads, highways, school buildings, courts, and parks.

What kinds of goods and services does the U.S. government buy?

Employing Workers

As a group, governments are the single largest employer in our economy. Although the numbers vary, in a recent year, about 16 percent of our workforce was made up of public employees. Police officers, firefighters, teachers, and sanitation workers are examples of public employees. Governments also employ administrative assistants, lawyers, data analysts, accountants, records clerks, department managers, maintenance technicians, and others.

From time to time, the government attempts to reduce the size of its workforce. However, citizens continue to demand more from their governments, and human resources must be added to meet these demands.

Raising Revenue

Governments must have money to be able to buy goods and services and hire and pay workers. Because governments provide goods and services, usually at no charge to the public, they must have other means of raising income.

Government income is referred to as its *revenue*. Taxes are a common method governments use to raise revenue. Tax policies are established to pay for the services provided. Taxes may be levied on earnings, property values, and the sale price of goods and services.

Your individual earnings are subject to both federal and state income taxes. Taxes on the earnings of individuals are the largest source of revenue for the federal government. Corporate income taxes, based on the business's profit, also provide a substantial amount of revenue for the federal government.

Local governments generally rely on a *property tax*, or revenue from taxes on real estate. This tax is based on the assessed value of land and buildings attached to the ground. Property tax revenues are used to fund schools and other government services. Both businesses and individuals pay this tax.

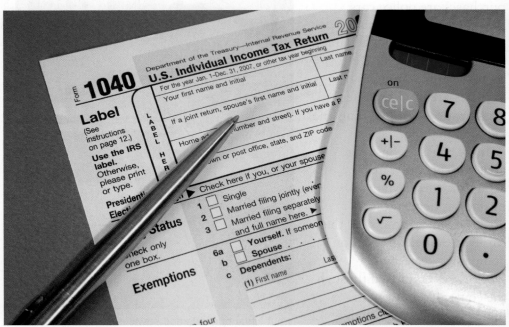

How does the U.S. government use the money collected from income taxes?

Sales tax, a state or local tax on the price of goods and services, is a major source of income for some cities, counties, and states. Sales taxes are collected by the seller and remitted later to the government. The business that sells the taxed good or service keeps a small part of what is collected to help pay for the expense of keeping records of the taxes collected.

Borrowing Money

Governments also have a frequent need to borrow money. When a government needs to build a new school, courthouse, or convention center, it may obtain the needed funds through borrowing.

A common form of government borrowing is through issuing bonds. If you buy local and state *government bonds*, also called *municipal bonds*, you are lending money to the government that issued the bond. The government becomes a debtor and pays you interest on the amount you have invested. Banks, insurance companies, and other financial institutions help finance governments by purchasing these bonds in large quantities. They sometimes resell the bonds in smaller units to businesses and individuals. Government bonds are a good form of investment for many individuals because they are considered less risky than other investments and are often exempt from federal, state, and local income taxes.

©John Clark, 2009/ Used under license from Shutterstock.com

Why does the U.S. government issue bonds?

The U.S. government also sells U.S. savings bonds. These bonds are available to purchase in various amounts. Bondholders earn a fixed rate of return, and the earnings are exempt from state and local income taxes.

TEAMWORK

Review the categories of taxes collected by local, state, and federal governments in your state. In each of those categories, identify the taxes that you and your parents must pay. In groups, discuss whether those taxes seem fair and whether or not as citizens you get your money's worth for the services provided by the governments. As a class, share and discuss your answers.

CheckPOINT

What are the four business activities governments perform?

_____

_____

_____

Think Critically

1. In most states today, the legal age to enter into a binding contract is 18, also called the "age of majority." Do you think this age is reasonable? If not, what do you think the age of majority should be?

_____

_____

2. You have come up with a very popular logo for your product. What might happen to your business if the government does not give you exclusive rights to use the logo?

_____

_____

3. Why do you think that bonds issued by the U.S. government are considered safer than bonds issued by corporations?

_____

_____

_____

Make Academic Connections

4. **Technology** Nearly all federal agencies and most state and local agencies have their own web pages that provide information and assistance for citizens seeking help. Access web pages for several government agencies, and write a sentence about what each contains.

_____

_____

_____

5. **Finance** Check advertisements and other sources of information for bonds, and note the difference in the interest rates for municipal bonds compared with bonds issued by corporations. Make a list of the bonds you find advertised and their comparative interest rates.

_____

_____

_____

6. **Business Law** Review the three types of intellectual property, and then identify three patented products, three copyrighted materials, and three trademarks. For each category, write a paragraph explaining why it is important for these products to be protected.

JUMP START

As part of her MBA program, Brittney was assigned a team project to develop a code of ethics for a local company. Brittney's team agreed to write a code of ethics for the Triad Bakery, which by now had almost 200 employees. Members of the team interviewed the three owners, as well as managers at all levels of the company. They concluded that the company expected all employees to be honest in their dealings with customers and suppliers and to treat customers with respect. Brianna and Emilio liked the code of ethics developed by Brittney's team and wanted to adopt it for their company. How should the partners go about distributing this guide to employees?

GOALS

Explain the importance of business ethics

Describe how businesses can be socially responsible

KEY TERMS

business ethics, p. 105

code of ethics, p. 106

bribe, p. 107

social responsibility, p. 108

©Andresr, 2009/ Used under license from Shutterstock.com

Business Ethics

Businesses are expected to operate ethically and to be socially responsible. The general public expects a business to be honest and fair in its business dealings and to help communities become better places in which to live. A business's good reputation helps to attract customers.

Most business leaders want their employees to be honest and fair in all business dealings. Ethical behavior on the part of those who represent a business can be a major factor in the success of the business.

Code of Ethics

Ethics are the principles of conduct governing an individual or group. **Business ethics** are rules about how businesses and their employees are expected to behave. Ethical behavior involves conforming to those rules. Unethical behavior violates those rules. In dealing with business ethics, a code of ethics can help a business identify proper behavior expected of all employees.

A **code of ethics** is a set of rules for guiding the actions of employees or members of an organization. Codes of ethics address topics such as protecting confidential business information, treating others with respect, and showing integrity in all business conducted. Once established, the code should be a guide of what is expected of all employees within that company. A sample code of ethics appears below.

The code should be worded in terms of acceptable behavior rather than in forbidden action. The guidelines for writing a code of ethics shown below are useful in drawing up the code.

1. Determine the purpose of the code.

2. Consider involving employees in writing the code.

3. Determine rules or principles to which all members of the organization will be expected to adhere.

4. Include information about how the code will be enforced.

5. Write the code to meet the needs and values of the organization.

6. Determine how the code will be implemented and where it will be published or posted.

7. Determine how and when the code will be reviewed.

Even with a well-developed code of ethics to guide employees, they may still encounter situations where making the right choice poses a dilemma.

CODE OF ETHICS

- We serve as ambassadors of goodwill for our company in all of our contacts.
- We keep the interests of our clients and customers first in all of our dealings.
- We settle for only high-quality effort and attainment in everything we do.
- We protect all company business information that is confidential.
- We value time and use it wisely, always focusing on tasks that benefit our company.
- We use company equipment and supplies for business use only.
- We recognize the importance of teamwork and strive to be effective members of our team.
- When disagreements arise, we will treat each other with respect and dignity.
- We will reject bribes, expensive gifts, or payments from any person or business with whom we do business.
- We will help our company to be socially responsible and will work to make our communities better places in which to live.
- We understand that any violation of this code of ethics will result in appropriate action being taken by an authority of the company.

Ethical Conduct

Top management should set a good example of ethical conduct for their employees. Executives and leaders who exhibit strong moral character and make ethical business decisions are important in setting an ethical standard of behavior for a business.

Putting codes of ethics into practice is not always easy. In some businesses, bribes may be demanded before a transaction can be completed. A **bribe** is a forced payment of money or a favor required before an official or decision maker will make a favorable decision. Bribery is illegal in the United States, but in other countries, it is legal. Doing business in those countries may require management to make difficult decisions.

A company must earn a reasonable profit, so it must remain competitive. To maintain a competitive edge while behaving ethically can be a challenge. Situations requiring ethical decision making could include the following.

- A business wants to expand into a profitable market in another country, but to do so, it must give expensive gifts to key government officials.

- A company discovers a minor defect in a popular and quite profitable product it is currently selling. Only the officials of the company know about the defect.

- Important, secret information about a competitor's product is given to top management by an employee who is a computer hacker.

Some companies concerned about ethical behavior have established educational programs on ethical conduct. Program topics range from dealing with business practices in other countries that differ from U.S. practices to reinforcing personal ethical standards such as not taking supplies and materials home for personal use. Employees are instructed on how to make ethical decisions on the job.

©Jozsef Szasz-Fabian, 2009/ Used under license from Shutterstock.com

Is bribery an ethical way to conduct business?

CheckPOINT
How does a code of ethics help to guide business behavior?
_____
_____

Social Responsibility

Another important concern of U.S. businesses is being socially responsible. **Social responsibility** refers to the duty of a business to contribute to the well-being of the community and society at large. When a company tries to be socially responsible, it must consider the interests and concerns of many groups. Some of the groups may have needs that conflict with each other. Common social concerns include protection of the environment, inclusion of minorities and women in the workplace, employment of physically challenged and older workers, and a safe and healthy work environment. In addition, U.S. businesses must practice social responsibility when conducting business globally.

Environmental Protection

Conservation is preserving scarce natural resources. It is a goal of many companies. Lumber companies, for instance, may plant trees to replace those they remove. Some mining companies restore the environment to its original condition after extracting raw materials. Whenever possible, environmentally responsible companies preserve or restore natural resources.

When the environment is contaminated with by-products of human activity, the result is *pollution*. Socially responsible businesses that cause pollution of lakes and rivers have taken action to eliminate or correct those operations. Green technologists and engineers are designing new equipment and systems to reduce waste and pollution that will help businesses in these efforts.

The federal government has set standards for water and air quality. These standards are monitored and enforced by the Environmental Protection Agency (EPA). Businesses and the EPA work closely together to develop alternatives and make the environment healthier.

The American Recovery and Reinvestment Act of 2009 will help encourage technological advancement in science and health. Investment in environmental protection and other infrastructure areas should provide long-term economic benefit. The EPA will manage $7 billion in projects and programs that should help achieve these goals.

Workplace Diversity

Businesses are increasingly sensitive to the roles of women, ethnic groups, the physically challenged, and older workers in the workplace. The workforce of

COMMUNICATE

A local factory that employs almost half the workforce in your small town has just received notice from the EPA that it is violating clean air standards. Write a letter to the business owner expressing your concern about the pollution. In your letter, suggest ways for the company to address its air pollution problem.

a business should reflect the various groups that constitute the community. Members of these groups must have equal access to education, training, jobs, and career advancement. A major challenge facing businesses today involves learning how to manage a workforce made up of workers who represent the diverse cultures in our society.

Another issue involves the removal of employment barriers, often referred to as *glass ceilings*, for women and minorities. Equal opportunity laws have eliminated sex-based job descriptions and requirements. Women and minorities today effectively perform in jobs once available only to white male workers. Employers have also taken steps to provide access for wheelchairs and other accommodations for those with sight or hearing limitations to meet the requirements of the Americans with Disabilities Act (ADA) and other legislation.

Other laws have eliminated bias against older workers. The Age Discrimination in Employment Act does not allow employers to use age as a basis for decisions in employment, promotions, or terminations. It protects persons aged 40 and older.

Job Safety

Having a safe place in which to work is important to all employees. They should be able to work in an office or factory free from risks that could cause accidents or illnesses. In addition to protection from physical harm, workers need to know how to deal with the unexpected. Safety also involves training in how to work safely and what to do in case of an emergency. To protect workers, most companies have put a variety of programs into practice, often in cooperation with the Occupational Safety and Health Administration (OSHA), a government agency that sets, regulates, and enforces safety standards.

The workplace is also being made healthier. Clauses that relate to employee well-being are often included in union contracts and company policy manuals. Some companies sponsor seminars on getting proper exercise, eating a balanced diet, and maintaining a healthy lifestyle. A healthy workforce is a productive workforce. Employees who have good health generally have fewer work absences, are more alert, and make fewer errors than other workers.

How can businesses improve job safety?

NETBookmark

Social responsibility refers to the duty of a business to contribute to the well-being of society. Ben & Jerry's Ice Cream is well known for its efforts to be a socially responsible business. Access www.cengage.com/school/business/21biz and click on the link for Chapter 4. Browse the Ben & Jerry's website and describe some examples of social responsibility you find there. (*Hint:* Click the *Activism* link on the home page.) Then follow the *Mission Statement* link and name the three components of the company's mission. Which do you consider the most important—or do you think all components are equally significant?

www.cengage.com/school/business/21biz

International Business Relationships

Many U.S. companies have operations in other countries. This can have a positive effect on another country's economy. However, while conducting business internationally, U.S. companies should comply with societal expectations and standards. They must act as good citizens and be aware of the other country's customs to avoid offensive actions. If U.S. companies have production facilities in another country, they should not pollute or harm the environment in any way.

Unfair labor practices, such as child labor, are often found in other countries. By working only with foreign businesses that adhere to fair labor standards, U.S. companies are operating in a socially responsible manner. U.S. businesses have a responsibility to operate in a way that benefits the other country and its citizens.

Social Responsibility Benefits and Costs

Businesses benefit from being socially responsible. It is good for their company image, it reduces the need for government actions against them, and it helps to improve the quality of life in the community. Today, more than ever, workers and consumers are aware of social responsibility among businesses.

While many businesses want to be socially responsible, they have to deal with the fact that social responsibility often involves costs that reduce profits. Money spent for nonpolluting technology, for building renovations to remove hazards, for wellness and rehabilitation programs, and for social projects are business expenses. Businesses contribute significantly to the economic life of a community. Yet to remain in business and continue to make such contributions, they must earn a profit.

Businesses that are not profitable will close their doors, will lay off employees, and may cause local economies to suffer. Striking a balance between being socially responsible and earning a reasonable profit is a challenge for businesses of all sizes.

CheckPOINT

What does the term "social responsibility" mean?

_____

_____

Think Critically

1. Why do businesses need to publish and distribute codes of ethics?

_____

_____

2. Why do you think some people do not behave ethically?

_____

_____

3. What will happen to the economy if nonrenewable natural resources are used up? What effect would this have on your life?

_____

_____

_____

4. If a business must decide between spending a large amount of money for new pollution-reduction technology or closing down, what issues must the business consider in its decision?

_____

_____

Make Academic Connections

5. **International Marketing** What are the major issues to consider in making ethical decisions in each of the following situations? What ethical decision would you make in each case?

a. Your company will have to give expensive gifts and provide lavish entertainment to key business and political leaders to participate in a very profitable market in Asia. Gifts and entertainment are contrary to your company's code of ethics.

_____

_____

b. To conduct business in a new South American market, you must agree to buy all raw materials from certain South American companies whose quality control is not assured. This action would take business away from some loyal U.S. suppliers.

_____

_____

_____

Chapter Summary

4.1 **International Business**
  A. Imports, exports, and international currencies are concerns in international business.
  B. Barriers to international trade include quotas, tariffs, and embargoes.

4.2 **Government in the U.S. Economy**
  A. The government protects businesses through regulations and laws concerning contracts, intellectual property rights, and utilities.
  B. The government buys goods and services, employs workers, raises revenue, and borrows money.

4.3 **Business Ethics and Social Responsibility**
  A. Ethics are principles of morality and rules of conduct. A code of ethics can help guide the activity of individuals within a company or an organization.
  B. Social responsibility is the duty of a business to contribute to the well-being of a community and society at large.

Vocabulary Builder

Choose the term that best fits the definition. Write the letter of the answer in the space provided. Some terms may not be used.

contract 1. An agreement to exchange goods and services for something of value

exports 2. Goods and services sold to other countries

bribe 3. A forced payment of money or a favor required before an official or decision maker will make a favorable decision

international Business 4. Business activities necessary for creating, shipping, and selling of goods and services across national borders

Business Ethics 5. Rules about how businesses and their employees are expected to behave

social responsibility 6. The duty of a business to contribute to the well-being of a community and society at large

code of Ethics 7. A set of rules for guiding the actions of employees or members of an organization

Embargo 8. An action taken to stop the import or export of goods and services completely

Balance of trade 9. The difference between a country's exports and imports

Quota 10. A limit on the quantity of a product that can be imported or exported

imports 11. Goods and services one country buys from other countries

intellectual property 12. A tax a government places on certain imported products to cause the price of that product to increase

a. balance of trade
b. bribe
c. business ethics
d. code of ethics
e. contract
f. embargo
g. exports
h. imports
i. intellectual property
j. international business
k. quota
l. social responsibility
m. tariff

Review Concepts

Point Your Browser
www.cengage.com/
school/business/21biz

13. What is a positive balance of trade? a negative balance of trade?

    Balance positive country's exports exceed its imports
    balance negative " imports " its exports

14. What does the phrase "exchange rate" mean?

    The value of one currency for the purpose of
    conversion to another.

15. What are three kinds of barriers to international trade?

    Tariffs, non-tariff barriers to trade, import
    licenses, export licenses, import quotas

16. What are the four basic elements of a contract? Describe each.

    Offer, acceptance,

17. Give at least two examples of intellectual property.

    utility patents, Design patents.

18. What are public utilities, and why do governments regulate them?

19. What is the most common way that governments raise revenue?

20. What are business ethics and why are they important?

21. What is meant by a business's social responsibility?

Apply What You Learned

22. Canada is the United States' major export partner. Why does the United States export so many goods and services to Canada?

_____

_____

_____

23. What are some political and social policies of a country that might cause another country to impose an embargo on its goods?

_____

_____

_____

24. Why is it important to read all the "fine print" when you enter into a contractual relationship?

_____

_____

_____

25. Would consumers be better off if all public utilities, including electric and gas companies, were deregulated so that the marketplace could set prices? Explain why or why not.

_____

_____

_____

_____

26. Why do you think governments constitute one of the major employers in the U.S. economy?

_____

_____

_____

27. Which tax do you think is fairer to citizens of a community, a sales tax or a property tax? Explain why.

_____

_____

_____

Make Academic Connections

28. **Business Math** Below is a list of costs of five imported products and the tariff on each one. For each product, compute the total cost by determining the tariff amount and adding it to the product cost.

Product	Cost	Tariff	Total Cost
a. perfume	$10	48%	_____
b. sweater	$60	25%	_____
c. television	$350	20%	_____
d. shoes	$80	60%	_____
e. automobile	$25,000	90%	_____

29. **Ecology** The tropical rain forests of the world are vital to the future of clean air throughout the planet. Yet these rain forests are being destroyed at the rate of around 50 million acres a day—that is the equivalent of 6,000 football fields per hour. Find some information on where these rain forests are located and what is being done to try to protect and preserve them. Write a two-page report about why the rain forests are being destroyed and what effect the continued destruction of rain forests may have on you.

30. **Business Law** Research the Americans with Disabilities Act. Find out some of the requirements of that act for employers and schools and how effective the act has been. Then summarize your findings in a short report.

31. **Careers** The glass ceiling is a reality in many companies. Look up information on that subject and write a brief paragraph on your findings and your thoughts on the issue.

Ethical Dilemma

32. A purchasing department employee must make a decision about which company to do business with for office supplies, materials, and equipment. One of the businesses under consideration gives that employee expensive gifts during the holidays and on other occasions. The employee says that receiving these gifts does not have an effect on the decision about which company to choose. Do you believe this employee? Could these gifts be considered a form of bribery? Do you think gift giving among businesses is ever ethical? Explain your answers.

_____

_____

_____

_____

_____

CHAPTER 5

The Role of Consumers

5.1 Consumer Information

5.2 Consumer Decisions

5.3 Consumer Rights and Responsibilities

Careers in Business

CONSUMERS UNION

Consumers Union is a nonprofit organization that provides information on consumer issues. It publishes *Consumer Reports*, a monthly magazine that contains results of its research and testing on consumer products. Along with testing products and informing the public, its basic mission is to empower consumers to protect themselves.

Policy analysts at Consumers Union research issues that affect consumers. They meet with Congress and the media concerning consumer-related public policy issues. Additional responsibilities include identifying opportunities for grassroots efforts and helping to build an activist base to promote public policy objectives, such as those for energy and environmental policies.

Policy analysts must have a college degree and a minimum of three years of experience working in legislative, regulatory, or nonprofit lobbying organizations. They need strong analytical and communication skills.

Think Critically

1. Which aspect of the policy analyst job at Consumers Union most interests you. Why?
2. Who do you think benefits from the work of policy analysts? Why?

PROJECT | Consumer Rights Campaign

Project Objectives

- Understand how to research consumer topics to make better-informed decisions
- Conduct a class campaign about consumer rights and responsibilities

©Andresr, 2009/ Used under license from Shutterstock.com

Getting Started

Read the Project Process below. Make a list of any materials you will need.

- Divide into six groups. Every group will prepare materials on the topics of the consumer "right to be informed" and "consumer responsibilities." Each group will be assigned one of the remaining six consumer rights.
- Groups will develop strategies for promoting awareness of their assigned topics—through posters, flyers, skits, the Internet, or other methods.

Project Process

5.1 Use the information sources listed in the chapter to research the topics assigned. Have each group member read one source and write a short summary on how it can be used to help make informed decisions.

5.2 Make a chart of the factors that influence the consumer decision-making process. In your chart, identify how each factor relates to your consumer rights and consumer responsibilities.

5.3 Using the information you gathered above, create posters, flyers, skits, web pages, and so forth for your topics. Use the most effective media for your message and your audience.

Chapter Review

Project Wrap-up After the group presentations, vote on the presentations for the "right to be informed" and "consumer responsibilities" to use in your class campaign. Present it to your school.

©Losevsky Pavel, 2009/ Used under license from Shutterstock.com

GOALS

Describe several sources of information for consumers

Explain how governments and businesses help consumers

KEY TERMS

consumer, p. 118

grade, p. 120

label, p. 122

 JUMP START

Brianna has been busy gathering information about new refrigeration units that she and Brittney need for one of their bakeries. She has visited several local stores and has made price and quality comparisons. She has read product labels, brochures, and warranties and talked with salespeople. Brianna has also visited the local library and checked out publications that have evaluations and ratings of consumer products. In addition, she has also used the Internet as a source of information. Why do you think Brianna is doing so much research before making a purchase?

Consumers and Information

[A **consumer** is a person or business that buys or uses goods and services.] Individuals and businesses consume products and buy services every day. They buy products such as food, clothing, and supplies. They pay for services such as car repair, haircuts, and medical attention.

Businesses provide consumers with a vast variety of goods and services. Consumers must make appropriate decisions as to which of these services and goods to buy. [Informed consumers gather information about products and services before making a buying decision.] Uninformed consumers may unnecessarily waste resources and make decisions that are harmful to the environment.

Consumers have the power to decide to buy or not to buy. So it is important for businesses to serve the needs of consumers. Without satisfied customers, a business would not make repeat sales, earn a profit, and stay in business.

When consumers have to make a decision about what to buy, there are many sources of information available to help them with their decision.

Product-Testing Organizations

Product-testing organizations test products and services for the benefit of consumers and businesses. Manufacturers pay these organizations to perform safety tests. Underwriters Laboratories, Inc., (UL) is one of the best-known product-testing organizations. UL labs test electrical components and products from all over the world for fire and electrical safety. The UL symbol indicates that the product has been tested and found to be safe for normal use.

Another product-testing organization is the Association of Home Appliance Manufacturers (AHAM). This association develops performance and safety standards for household appliances, including use and care information. When the AHAM seal of approval is given to a product, it means the product has been tested and has met the organization's standards.

Print Publishers

Some organizations print scientific, technical, and educational information about products and services. Some, such as Consumers Union, are nonprofit organizations that perform independent tests on consumer goods and publish articles on the quality of the goods. Consumers Union publishes its findings in a monthly magazine called *Consumer Reports*.

Good Housekeeping and *Parents* magazines, which are for-profit publications, provide articles and product information. *Good Housekeeping* contains endorsements of products that have been tested and meet the magazine's standards. The Good Housekeeping Seal lets consumers know that a product has been tested and approved. This seal includes a promise that the magazine will replace the product if found to be defective within two years of purchase. *Consumers Digest* is another for-profit publication that provides consumer information.

In the area of finance, periodicals such as *Money*, *Kiplinger's Personal Finance*, and *Fortune* evaluate and report on the performance of stocks, bonds, mutual funds, and other investments. Specialty magazines and newspapers provide information about specific kinds of products and services, such as cars, computers, cell phones, and electronics. Information provided can also help consumers understand technical or complex products and services.

Broadcast Organizations

Radio and television are also sources of helpful consumer information. Many stations carry regular programs that inform the public about product safety, care and use of products, and shopping tips. Some broadcast talk shows are designed to help listeners with their consumer problems. Radio and TV programs that intervene on behalf of the consumer can be quite effective in resolving problems.

The Internet

Online information has become a valuable resource for consumers. Most consumer information publications and sources can be accessed through the Internet. *Good Housekeeping* reportedly is the most trusted online source of advice about home, food, diet, nutrition, and women's health. Other websites, such as Epinions.com, ConsumerSearch.com, and Angie's List, are dedicated to supplying consumer product and service reviews. Through use of a search engine, consumers can obtain answers to questions about consumer issues.

CheckPOINT

Why should consumers do research before making a purchase?

_____

_____

Consumer Information from Government and Businesses

Government agencies provide useful consumer information. So do businesses that produce and market goods and services.

Information from the Government

Federal, state, and local governments help citizens become informed consumers. The Federal Citizen Information Center (FCIC) serves as the federal government's headquarters for consumer information. This center issues the Consumer Information Catalog, which lists a number of publications of special interest to consumers. The center also publishes the results of government research and product tests and maintains a website to assist consumers.

The United States Department of Agriculture (USDA) publishes information about food. This agency provides information that helps consumers judge quality, buy wisely, improve shopping practices, plan meals, and improve nutrition. Inspecting and grading food is an important service of the USDA. A grade is a rating given to food that indicates the quality or size of the product.

Other federal government agencies that provide consumer information include the Federal Trade Commission (FTC), Food and Drug Administration (FDA), Consumer Product Safety Commission (CPSC), National Highway Traffic Safety Administration (NHTSA), Department of Housing and Urban Development (HUD), and Environmental Protection Agency (EPA).

Every state has consumer protection agencies. These agencies have websites to provide information and handle consumer questions. Large cities and counties also have consumer assistance offices.

DID YOU KNOW ?

In one holiday season, the FTC penalized seven well-known e-tailers for violating mail or telephone order rules. The companies paid $1.5 million in penalties.

Tech Literacy

GOVERNMENT PROTECTS ONLINE SHOPPERS

Online shoppers are protected by federal laws that govern purchases made through the Internet. "E-tailers" (Internet retailers) must ship an order within their advertised time frames or within 30 days of the receipt of the order. If there is a delay, they must inform the buyer and give a revised shipping date. The e-tailer must allow the buyer to agree to the delay or cancel the order and receive a prompt refund. Consumers must also be alert to deceptive mail-in rebate practices. E-tailers must display: (1) the type of rebate offered, (2) the details of the terms of the offer, and (3) the total price consumers must pay at the time of the purchase to receive the rebate.

THINK CRITICALLY

Why does the government regulate Internet purchases? Do you think these laws are good safeguards for online shopping? Why or why not?

Information from Businesses

As a public service and in an effort to sell goods and services, businesses make information available to consumers. Some businesses provide booklets on a variety of consumer topics. Banks and insurance companies often publish materials that help consumers manage their money. Some retailers provide materials that help consumers with buying decisions and give tips on improving buying skills. In addition to print materials, information from businesses is presented in the form of advertising, product labels, customer service departments, and Better Business Bureaus.

Advertising The most widely available source of consumer information provided by businesses is advertising. The main purpose of advertising is to convince you to buy a product or service, so you must use it with caution. Useful advertising gives facts that you can use to compare a product with

How does advertising benefit consumers?

TEAMWORK

Work with a partner to role-play a scenario in which a dissatisfied customer visits the customer service department of a store. Role-play the customer and customer service representative. Create the details of the purchase, problem, and solution. Perform the scenario in class.

NETBookmark

Garment manufacturers are required to provide instructions to consumers for the care of apparel. Many clothing labels show these instructions as symbols. Access www.cengage.com/school/business/21biz and click on the link for Chapter 5. The Apparelsearch.com website includes a page of care label symbols. Examine the symbols, and then select one and see if you can guess what it means. Then click the symbol. Did you guess correctly? Why do you think apparel manufacturers give care instructions on clothing labels in symbol format?

www.cengage.com/school/business/21biz

another. It tells you what the product is, how it is made, and what it will do. Be sure that general terms, such as "better" or "the best," are backed up with evidence.

"Word of mouth" by satisfied customers is an informal and useful means of advertising. Although individual tastes and preferences need to be considered, positive information from a consumer who has used a product can be a reliable source of information. Caution, however, is recommended when reading Internet testimonials.

Product Labels A label is a tag attached to or printed on a product that contains useful information about it. Labels may tell what the product is made of, its size, how to care for it, and when and where it was made. Clothing labels must give instructions for washing or cleaning.

Customer Service Departments Many businesses set up special departments to provide information and service to customers. Consumers call or visit these departments to report problems with purchases they have made or services that have not been delivered or completed satisfactorily. Customer service departments also offer general assistance, such as answering questions and handling returns. They may provide customers with booklets on a range of consumer topics.

Better Business Bureaus In an effort to improve credibility, businesses have joined together in a self-regulation effort and created Better Business Bureaus (BBBs). These bureaus are franchised, and businesses become accredited members by committing to the BBB standards and paying yearly membership dues. Accredited members are known for their reliability and integrity. BBBs work to maintain ethical business practices and to combat consumer fraud. They are frequent sources of news for the media about scams, alerts on frauds, and consumer issues.

Better Business Bureaus can provide helpful information about businesses. If consumers have a problem with a business, they may file a complaint with a BBB. All complaints filed are available to the public. The bureaus only give out facts. They do not recommend products, companies, or charities.

CheckPOINT

Why are product labels necessary?

_____

_____

Think Critically

1. Why should consumers look for product-testing organization symbols or seals of approval on products before they make a purchase?

_____

_____

_____

2. Why do you think that radio and TV stations are effective in helping consumers resolve their problems with businesses?

_____

_____

_____

_____

3. Why do you think that the federal government has agencies and centers that help consumers?

_____

_____

_____

_____

4. Which of the ways in which businesses help consumers do you think is the most useful? How would you use that help if you needed it?

_____

_____

_____

_____

Make Academic Connections

5. **Business Literature** Locate copies of at least three of the publications mentioned in this lesson. After reading through them, write one or two sentences about your impression of each publication.

6. **Consumerism** One of the pioneers and noted leaders in the consumer movement is Ralph Nader. Do some research on Mr. Nader to find out what he has done in terms of helping consumers. Write a one-page report of your findings. Conclude with a statement as to whether or not you believe Mr. Nader has been good for consumers and businesses.

©Monkey Business Images, 2009/ Used under license from

GOALS

Identify wise buying strategies

Describe what to consider when making wise buying decisions

KEY TERMS

comparison shopping, p.124

unit price, p. 125

brand name, p. 127

impulse buying, p. 129

JUMP START

Brittney takes her consumer role very seriously. Comparison shopping is something she enjoys and does often. She uses her business decision-making skills in the process. When her car was no longer reliable, she shopped for a new one. She visited several dealerships that had good reputations. She checked information and prices in magazines and on the Internet. She felt comfortable making her decision. She also applies her decision-making skills to smaller purchases such as food and clothing. Her math skills and ability to compute data help her make sound decisions on which products are the best buy. What, besides price, should Brittney consider when making purchase decisions?

Wise Buying Strategies

The business decision-making process can be applied to making wise decisions as a consumer. You begin by identifying your needs or wants. Then you learn what choices are available regarding price, quality, and variety. Following that, you determine how much you are willing to pay and the quality you desire. After you've considered the alternatives, you make your decision.

Good buying strategies involve comparison shopping—that is, comparing unit prices, quality, and services associated with one product with those of another. It also involves giving consideration to promotions and sales. Comparison shopping will make you a better consumer and will result in greater value for the money you spend. Except for utilities or highly specialized goods, very few products are made or sold by only one business.

Compare Unit Prices

A **unit price** is a price per unit of measure, such as price per ounce, pound, quart, or other unit of measure. To calculate a unit price, you divide the total price of the item by the number of units of measure in the item. Comparing the unit price of two items tells you which is the better buy. Some shoppers carry a pocket calculator with them to compute unit costs. Unit prices are often posted on the store shelves where the products are stocked.

Compare Quality

You want to get your money's worth when you buy something. As a wise consumer, you need to compare the quality of similar products. High-quality merchandise and services normally cost more. However, buying lower-quality items sometimes can turn out to be more expensive if the item wears out in a shorter period of time or needs more repairs and adjustments. For instance, Hiroto bought a low-quality pair of hiking boots at a cheaper price. They soon wore out, and he had to buy a second pair. A higher-quality pair of boots costing more would have lasted as long or longer than the two pairs he bought.

Compare Services

A wise buyer compares services offered by businesses. Most businesses try to give good service. However, types of services differ. Some businesses sell for cash only. Others extend credit as a service. Some businesses deliver goods for no extra charge. Others charge for delivery. Some serve customers by keeping a large stock of merchandise from which to choose. Others stock fewer items.

Service of any kind is important, but you should not pay for more service than you need. Merchants who sell on credit incur a cost in handling credit sales. If they accept credit cards, they might pay 4 percent of their credit sales to the credit company. Merchants who accept only cash may pass the savings on to their customers.

Business Math Connection

Calculate the unit price for a 16-ounce bag of frozen vegetables that costs $3.36 and an 8-ounce bag that costs $1.92. Determine the better buy.

SOLUTION
The formula for calculating unit price is

	Total price of item	÷	Number of units in item	=	Unit price
16-oz. bag:	$3.36	÷	16 ounces	=	$0.21
8-oz. bag:	$1.92	÷	8 ounces	=	$0.24

The 16-ounce bag is less expensive per ounce.

Consider Sales

Have you ever noticed that some stores have a "sale" all the time? The word "sale" is perhaps the most overused, and least trusted, term in marketing. When an item is truly on sale, it is offered at a price lower than its normal selling price. Retailers generally have three types of sales: promotional, clearance, and special-purchase sales.

A *promotional sale* often occurs when a new store is opening or when a store moves to a new location and wants to attract customers. This type of sale can also be used to build acceptance for a new product or service. Consumers often get good buys for their money at these sales.

Stores use *clearance sales* to sell merchandise they no longer wish to carry in stock. Clearance sales may occur at the end of a season or may include odd sizes or out-of-date merchandise. There are bargains to be found in clearance sales, but you must be certain you really need what is being sold.

Special-purchase sales feature goods that a retailer purchases from a manufacturer who is overstocked, goods that no longer are made, or stock from a company that is going out of business. The retailer offers this special-purchase merchandise at considerably reduced prices. Bargains are available, but as always, selections must be made carefully.

CheckPOINT

What strategies are involved in wise buying?

_____

_____

Wise Buying Decisions

The business environment in the U.S. economy is very competitive. Businesses will try to get a competitive edge through one means or another. For consumers, that means there will be a great variety of goods and services available. A business's reputation, brand names, types of store, and timing are factors consumers need to consider when making a buying decision.

Business Reputation

Business owners readily acknowledge that the most valuable business asset is a good reputation. The wise business owner knows that a satisfied customer is likely to return and even recommend the business to friends. Businesses with good reputations have salespeople who know the uses and the quality of the goods they sell. They are concerned about matching the right goods with the customers' needs. When you buy from a business with a good reputation, you can usually rely on its salespeople to help you make wise selections.

Brand Names

A **brand name** is given to a product or service to distinguish it from other similar products or services. Brand names are created by the business that manufactures and sells the good or service. They are often used in national advertising campaigns. Clothing, shoes, tools, and cosmetics are among the goods sold largely based on brand names.

Recognizing brand names can help you as a consumer. You can usually expect uniform quality regardless of which store sells the item. Some well-known brands include Nike, Dell, The Gap, and L'Oreal.

Some stores have their own brand names, called *store brands* or *private brands*. For example, Craftsman has long been one of the brand names on tools sold by Sears. Store brands are usually sold at a lower price than national brands. Buying store brands may save you money while offering good quality.

Some stores offer generic products. A generic product is less expensive because it does not require advertising and may not be in a fancy package. Labels on generic products identify the contents so that comparisons can be made with the brand-name products. The minor differences in quality and uniformity between generic and brand-name products sometimes make these items a good value.

Types of Stores

When deciding where to buy, consumers have a wide variety of choices. To buy general merchandise, you can shop at department stores, discount stores, and specialty stores. In addition, specialty superstores, warehouse clubs, and factory outlets are available to consumers in many cities. In food retailing, there are supermarkets and convenience stores. Another alternative for shoppers is non-store shopping.

Department stores offer an extensive variety of goods and emphasize customer service. They are likely to offer personal shoppers, delivery, and wrapping of gifts.

©Philip Lange, 2009/ Used under license from Shutterstock.com

Why are there so many different types of stores?

Discount stores emphasize low prices, but most base their success on a high volume of sales rather than service. When service is not important, discount stores can be a good place to shop.

Specialty stores have a special, narrower line of products for sale, such as sporting goods, jewelry, or women's shoes. Consumers are attracted by the wide variety of selection within the product line. *Specialty superstores* offer low prices and a wide variety of a limited product line. These include retailers such as OfficeMax, Home Depot, and Best Buy.

Factory-outlet stores get products direct from the factory and sell them at lower prices. Their merchandise may be high quality, or it may have minor flaws, so careful inspection of products is important.

A *warehouse club* is a no-frills outlet that emphasizes the sale of large quantities of items at somewhat lower prices. Products are displayed in simple settings resembling a warehouse. Costco and Sam's Club are examples of this kind of store.

In food retailing, there are two types of stores. *Supermarkets* are large, full-service stores that carry a wide variety of national, store, and generic brands at moderate prices. In addition, many of these stores offer services such as banking and pharmaceuticals. *Convenience stores* are small stores that are open long hours and emphasize the sale of popular food items in an easily accessible location. Consumers usually pay higher prices for the convenience of getting in and out quickly.

A final option for consumers is non-store shopping, including mail order, vending machines, the Internet, and television shopping. Mail-order catalogs have been popular for many decades and continue to be popular today. Vending machines offer ease and convenience in purchasing small items. The Internet and television both offer endless opportunities to purchase goods and services from merchants and individual entrepreneurs.

Timing

Timing is one key to making wise purchases. Wise consumers take time to plan purchases and buy at the right time. They avoid buying on impulse and are efficient, saving time, energy, and money by planning. This often means slowing down, visiting more stores, and looking for the best values. You should avoid being hurried into buying anything. Buy what you need and want at the price you think is best.

When you make your purchase also can be important. Wise consumers know the right time to make their purchases to get the best prices. Some goods and services are sold at reduced prices during certain seasons or under certain conditions. Here are a few examples.

- Fresh fruits and vegetables at their peak growing seasons are usually sold at lower prices.

- Automobiles usually are cheaper at the end of the model year, generally in September before new models come out.

- Winter clothing is often on sale in January.

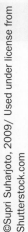

How can you avoid impulse buying?

Consumer magazines, newspaper articles, radio and television programs, the Internet, and other resources for consumers help identify times of the year when prices for products are reduced.

Wise consumers avoid **impulse buying**, which is buying without giving much thought to the purchase. Checkout lanes in supermarkets have impulse items attractively displayed within easy reach of customers waiting in line. Impulse buying can be harmful. Buying expensive items on impulse can be costly, resulting in consumers acquiring things they really do not want or need and having less to spend on what they do need.

The best values are gained by collecting information about an item and then carefully shopping for it. If you want to be an efficient shopper who gets the best value for your money, keep these three steps in mind.

1. Plan your purchases carefully. A consumer with a list makes better decisions when shopping and is less likely to buy on impulse. Shoppers can save money with a list whether it is for groceries, hardware, or clothing.

2. Use the available resources in planning your shopping. Conduct research to get the information you need, check out available services, and find out if what you want is available. The Internet now makes it easy to do comparison shopping in the convenience of your home.

3. Plan the route of your shopping trip to save time and fuel or bus fees. Unnecessary travel adds to the cost of your purchases.

Check**POINT**

Why might you choose a brand-name product over a generic product?

_____

_____

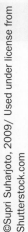

Think Critically

1. Why do you think it is important to be a wise consumer?

_____

_____

_____

2. What are some challenges consumers encounter when attempting to practice wise buying strategies?

_____

_____

_____

3. Why do you think it is difficult for today's consumers to take the time necessary to do comparison shopping?

_____

_____

_____

4. What do you think is the advantage of department stores over specialty stores? Which do you prefer when shopping, and why?

_____

_____

_____

_____

Make Academic Connections

5. **Advertising** Select three advertisements from magazines or newspapers. Study them, and then write a report answering these questions: What is each ad's basic appeal? What facts about the products or services are stated? What questions do you have after studying the ads? Attach a copy of each advertisement to your report.

6. **Business Math** For each of the following items, compute the unit price.
   A. 26-oz. can of soup @ $2.33 _____
   B. 18-oz. jar of applesauce @ $1.98 _____
   C. 3.7-lb. roast @ $11.03 _____
   D. 15-oz. box of cereal @ $3.52 _____
   E. 24-oz. box of raisins @ $4.30 _____
   F. 0.8 pound of cheese @ $3.59 _____

JUMP START

Emilio was upset about a smart phone he purchased about three months ago at a large electronics store. He had various problems when using the phone. Each time he returned to the store and explained the problems, the service department seemed to correct them, but they would always reoccur. It became obvious that this expensive product was not of the quality that he expected. The store's representatives said that they could not do anything more for him. Emilio made a list of the problems that occurred over the previous three months. Then he made an appointment to meet with the store owner. He presented his sales receipt and the list of problems. The owner agreed that there had to be some basic defects in the device. She contacted the manufacturer, and a replacement for the smart phone was sent to Emilio. Did Emilio act responsibly? Did the retailer act responsibly? Why or why not?

GOALS

State the seven rights in the Consumer Bill of Rights

Name five consumer responsibilities

KEY TERMS

consumer movement, p. 132

fraud, p. 132

monopoly, p. 133

©Cedric Carter, 2009/ Used under license from Shutterstock.com

Your Consumer Rights

In a market economy, businesses and consumers interact in selling and buying goods and services. In most business transactions, buyers and sellers are satisfied. However, not all businesses are honest and reputable. When a problem arises, consumers have both rights and responsibilities.

The pleasant relationship consumers desire with businesses does not always exist. Some businesses try to take advantage of consumers. They may make false claims about products. They may set unreasonably high prices. Or they may sell unsafe or ineffective products.

To help correct unfair business practices, consumers have organized and taken steps to get assistance. The uniting of consumers to get fair treatment from businesses is known as the **consumer movement**. The consumer movement led to the creation of some public and private consumer agencies. It also resulted in consumer protection policies and laws.

The Consumer Bill of Rights

One outgrowth of the consumer movement was President John F. Kennedy's presentation in 1962 of the Consumer Bill of Rights. This document declared the following consumer rights.

1. *Right to be informed*—to be given correct information needed to make an informed choice

2. *Right to safety*—to be protected from goods and services that are hazardous to health or life

3. *Right to choose*—to be assured of the availability of a variety of goods and services at competitive prices

4. *Right to be heard*—to be assured that consumer interests will be fully considered when laws are being written and enforced

Three other rights were added by later presidents.

5. *Right to a remedy*—to be assured of the right to legal correction of wrongs committed against consumers (Richard M. Nixon, 1969)

6. *Right to consumer education*—to have access to programs and information that help consumers make better economic decisions (Gerald R. Ford, 1975)

7. *Right to service*—to be entitled to convenience, courtesy, and responsiveness to problems and needs (William J. Clinton, 1994)

Right to Be Informed

You have the right to know what a product or service is and what it will do for you. **Fraud** occurs when consumers are given false information deliberately in an effort to make a sale. If a salesperson knowingly sells you a car on which the odometer has been turned back 30,000 miles, fraud has occurred.

You cannot expect all product information to be perfectly accurate, however. For instance, if a used-car salesperson said you could get 25 miles per gallon with a car you purchased and you get only 20 miles per gallon, this would not be considered fraud. No guarantee of that mileage was made.

©PaulPaladin, 2009/ Used under license from Shutterstock.com

Why do you think consumers have the right to be informed?

Being informed is the first line of defense against fraud. It can help you make well-informed decisions.

The Federal Trade Commission also protects your right to be informed by regulating advertising to ensure it contains informative and truthful statements. If you are misled by false statements when making a purchase, you can complain directly to this agency.

Right to Safety

You have a right to be safe from harm when using products or services. Agencies that work to ensure the safety of consumers include

- The Consumer Product Safety Commission (CPSC), which protects the public from unreasonable risks or injury from thousands of consumer products. It sets standards and recalls dangerous products from the market.

- The Food and Drug Administration (FDA), which promotes and protects the nation's public health. It regulates and supervises the safety of many products, including food, drugs, medical devices, and cosmetics.

- The U.S. Department of Agriculture (USDA), which sets quality standards for farm products to help ensure consumer safety. It also supervises the processing, inspection, and labeling of meat products and assigns grades of quality.

Right to Choose

One of the main activities of the Federal Trade Commission (FTC) is to prevent one company from using unfair practices to force competing companies out of business. When a business has no competition and controls the market for a good or service, it is said to have a **monopoly**. By driving away competition, monopolies limit your right to choose.

Cross-Cultural Relationships

CONSUMER PROTECTION IN ESTONIA

Estonia is one of the Balkan states that received freedom from Russia in 1994. Because Estonia was no longer a controlled economy, its businesses and consumers could participate in a free market. In 2005, Estonia established the European Consumer Education Centre of Estonia. It set up a Consumer Complaints Committee and established consumer protection through a Consumer Protection Board. The Board has three important functions: to supervise the consumer market, to settle consumer complaints, and to inform and advise consumers. There are also nongovernmental Consumer Associations that advise and assist consumers and protect the collective interests of consumers.

Think Critically

Was it wise for Estonia to establish a Consumer Protection Board? Why or why not? Why are nongovernmental associations also important?

©Diego Cervo, 2009/ Used under license from Shutterstock.com

How can consumers exercise their right to be heard?

Right to Be Heard

Businesses usually want to take care of problems that consumers have with their products or services. They may have a customer service department or one person designated to handle complaints.

In addition to voicing concerns with businesses, consumers can file complaints with the FTC's Bureau of Consumer Protection. The Bureau works to protect consumers against unfair, deceptive, or fraudulent practices by enforcing a variety of consumer protection laws. It represents the interests of consumers, develops consumer education materials, and contributes to actions of the FTC that could have an impact on consumers.

State governments, through their Attorneys General and Offices of Consumer Affairs, also take action to help and protect consumers. Better Business Bureaus can be contacted if your consumer rights have been violated. After you put your complaint in writing, the Bureau usually contacts the business involved and tries to help mediate the dispute.

Right to a Remedy

Your right to have action taken to correct a problem is protected by several laws. These laws include the Fair Packaging and Labeling Act, National Traffic and Motor Vehicle Safety Act, Truth in Labeling Act, and Fair Debt Collection Practices Act. These laws and others provide assurances that you can go to court to seek a legal remedy if, as a consumer, you have been wronged and cannot settle the matter out of court.

Consumers also have protection through a guarantee. A *guarantee* is a promise by the manufacturer or dealer, usually in writing, that a product is of a certain quality. It may promise that the product will be replaced if a problem, that is not the result of misuse, occurs during a specified period of time.

Guarantees are sometimes called express warranties. An *express warranty* is made orally or in writing and promises a specific quality of performance. It is wise to review any guarantee before buying. It is your right to require the business to put in writing any guarantee that has been offered orally. Written guarantees are important if you need to return a faulty product. It is important to read a guarantee thoroughly to find out exactly what is covered and for what period of time.

A guarantee that is imposed by law and is understood to apply even though it has not been stated is an *implied warranty*. It is assumed that the product being sold will meet an ordinary buyer's expectations and that the product is what it says it is. For example, it is implied that an over-the-counter health care product you take from a shelf at a pharmacy will not harm you when carefully selected and used according to directions.

DID YOU KNOW ❓

All 50 states have "lemon laws" to protect car buyers from purchasing cars with defects.

Right to Consumer Education

Consumer education programs focus on the interaction of consumers and producers. The buying decisions of consumers are important to themselves and their families. Educated consumers know that their decisions have an effect not only on their own lifestyles but also on the overall economy. Informed consumers are good for businesses and also good for the economy.

Right to Service

Consumers should be able to expect convenience, courtesy, and responsiveness to consumer problems and needs. The consumer right to service is also important to businesses. Businesses that take steps to ensure that their products and services meet stated quality and performance standards are those that become the most successful over time.

CheckPOINT

What does the right to a remedy help ensure?

_____

_____

TEAMWORK

Margarita bought an expensive purse at a boutique. Less than a month later, the zipper broke and one of the seams started to come apart. She knows that she overstuffed the purse several times but is unhappy and feels the boutique did not sell her a quality purse. Work in groups to decide on possible courses of action by Margarita. Regroup as a class and select the best course of action.

Your Consumer Responsibilities

Consumers are protected by hundreds of laws, and there are many agencies that look after their rights. Yet consumer problems are common. Just as some businesses have not met their responsibilities to consumers, some consumers are not always careful to meet their own consumer responsibilities. That can lead to difficulties. Consumers have a responsibility to be honest, reasonable, active, informed, and involved.

Be Honest

As a responsible consumer, you must be as honest with a business as you want it to be with you. Most consumers are honest, yet there are those who shoplift and think little of it. Taking a small item may seem harmless, but shoplifting anything is a crime. It is also a business expense. Shoplifting losses are estimated to be in the billions of dollars each year. Businesses make up for those losses by charging higher prices.

Some consumers are dishonest in other ways. For example, not telling a cashier that she gave you too much change or that she forgot to charge you for an item is dishonest. Dishonesty results in higher prices for all consumers.

Be Reasonable

It is important to complain when something is wrong with a product or service you have purchased. But make sure that something really is wrong before you complain. When you are certain there is a problem, make your complaint in a reasonable way with a complete explanation of what is wrong.

Present the details with a positive attitude, assuming the problem will be taken care of properly. Becoming hostile will not help the situation and often delays the desired solution. If you cannot get satisfactory action, it is proper to take your complaint to the owner or an officer of the business. It is also proper to write to a consumer agency or a Better Business Bureau if you do not receive satisfaction. Being businesslike in presenting your case will help you get the solution you desire. In most cases, a business will be glad to correct the problem because it will not want to lose you as a customer.

Be Active

Reporting unethical business practices is an activity you should participate in as a responsible consumer. It is important to report unethical business practices to prevent other consumers from becoming victims in similar situations. By reporting the matter to a consumer agency, you might be able to get the business to keep its word both to you and to future customers. A business community will not approve of unethical behavior by a business.

Be Informed

Just having the right to be informed will not make you an informed consumer. You must find and use the information available to you. Knowing about laws and consumer agencies that protect your rights and knowing how to handle violations of those rights will make your consumer role much more effective. Although staying informed is hard work, the extra effort will help you get better value for your money.

Be Involved

In your citizen role, your votes can put into office those who are concerned with consumer rights. As a consumer, you should make your concerns known to elected government officials and to consumer advocate agencies. Your involvement helps governments and agencies perform their functions and pass appropriate laws that help consumers and businesses.

CheckPOINT

As a consumer, why is it your responsibility to be active?

_____

_____

Think Critically

1. Which of the rights in the Consumer Bill of Rights do you think is the most important, and why?

   _____

   _____

2. What are some things that a salesperson could say about a product that are not necessarily true but would not constitute fraud?

   _____

   _____

3. Why do you think it is necessary for the Federal Trade Commission to regulate advertising?

   _____

   _____

   _____

4. Why is shoplifting a business expense, and why does it increase the prices of other items?

   _____

   _____

   _____

Make Academic Connections

5. **Business Law** The Sherman Antitrust Act of 1890 was enacted in an effort to regulate monopolies. Do some research on this law. Write a paragraph about some of its provisions, and state whether or not you think the law has been effective.

6. **English Composition** After reading the following situation, write a business letter to the Federal Trade Commission explaining the problem on behalf of Yoko.

   Yoko Nishimura read an advertisement about a product that would take away some pain she was experiencing. The ad said that satisfaction was guaranteed, that money would be refunded if the product did not relieve pain, and that no side effects would occur. Yoko bought the product through the mail. She used it exactly as the instructions said, but it did not relieve her pain in any way. She also developed a rash from using it. Yoko has telephoned and sent letters to the company. She returned the product along with her written complaint, but the company refuses to acknowledge her complaint and will do nothing about it.

Chapter Summary

5.1 Consumer Information

A. Consumer organizations help provide information needed by consumers. These organizations test products, publish magazines, and award seals of approval. Some organizations publish magazines with consumer tips.

B. The federal government provides a variety of materials for consumers. Businesses provide consumer information through print materials, advertising, product labels, customer service departments, and Better Business Bureaus.

5.2 Consumer Decisions

A. Comparison shopping and unit prices are important to consumer buying decisions. Quality and services need to be compared, and types of sales should be considered.

B. When you make a purchase, a business's reputation, brand names, types of stores, and timing also must be considered.

5.3 Consumer Rights and Responsibilities

A. The Consumer Bill of Rights includes the right to be informed, right to safety, right to choose, right to be heard, right to a remedy, right to consumer education, and right to service.

B. Consumers have the responsibility to be honest, reasonable, active, informed, and involved.

Vocabulary Builder

Choose the term that best fits the definition. Write the letter of the answer in the space provided.

__F__ 1. The rating given to food that indicates the quality or size of the product

__J__ 2. The price per unit of measure

__G__ 3. Buying without giving much thought to the purchase

__E__ 4. When consumers are given false information in an effort to make a sale

__D__ 5. The uniting of consumers to get fair treatment from businesses

__C__ 6. A person or business that buys or uses goods and services

__I__ 7. A business that has no competition and controls the market for a good or service

__A__ 8. A name given to a product or service to distinguish it from other similar products or services

__B__ 9. Comparing unit prices, quality, and services associated with one product with those of another

__H__ 10. A tag attached to or printed on a product that gives useful information about it

a. brand name

b. comparison shopping

c. consumer

d. consumer movement

e. fraud

f. grade

g. impulse buying

h. label

i. monopoly

j. unit price

Review Concepts

Point Your
Browser
www.cengage.com/
school/business/21biz

11. What is a consumer?

_____

_____

12. What are the four basic types of consumer information sources?

Right to safety, Right to be informed, Right to choose, Right to be heard.

13. Name several government agencies that provide consumer information.

_____

_____

_____

_____

14. What is the main purpose of advertising?

_____

_____

_____

15. What is the purpose of a Better Business Bureau?

_____

_____

_____

16. Describe comparison shopping in your own words.

_____

_____

_____

17. What is a unit price, and how does it help consumers when shopping?

_____

_____

_____

18. Why should a consumer consider a business's reputation when he or she makes a buying decision?

_____

_____

_____

_____

19. What are the eight types of stores?

_____

_____

20. Why is timing a factor in making a wise buying decision?

_____

_____

21. How does a monopoly interfere with your right to choose?

_____

_____

Apply What You Learned

22. Why is it necessary for independent organizations to test products made by manufacturers?

_____

_____

_____

_____

23. What are some precautions you should take when reading advertising as a source of consumer information?

_____

_____

_____

24. Do unit prices sometimes cause people to buy in larger quantities than they really need? Why or why not?

_____

_____

25. Do you think the Consumer Bill of Rights is necessary? Why or why not?

_____

_____

26. Why do you think that state Attorney General offices offer assistance to consumers in the marketplace?

_____

_____

_____

Make Academic Connections

27. **Research** Many consumer organizations have websites on the Internet. Locate the websites of five consumer organizations and write a paragraph on what you learn about each one.

28. **Business Services** Research the Better Business Bureau that serves your area. Find out about its history and how it has helped consumers. Try to locate someone who has used the Bureau, and ask him or her about the experience. Write a one-page report on your findings.

29. **Business Math** The following items and prices were on the shelf of a grocery store. Compute the unit price for each item.
    A. 12-oz. package of carrots @ $1.69 _____
    B. 3 lbs. chicken tenders @ $7.99 _____
    C. 12-oz. package of pork sausages @ $2.39 _____
    D. 4.68-lb. box of dishwasher detergent @ $6.99 _____
    E. 64-oz. bag of pinto beans @ $5.65 _____

30. **Advertising** Look through newspapers and find one advertisement for each of the following types of sales: promotional, clearance, and special-purchase. Write one or two sentences about each ad in terms of what it highlights and your reaction to it. Attach the ads to your paper.

31. **Ecology** "Green products" are goods manufactured or packaged in an environmentally friendly way. Since this is another way to help sell products, this has led to an increase in the number of green products on the market. Identify three products or packages that are environmentally friendly, and write a sentence describing each product or package.

32. **Business Law** Some products and services are sold with a guarantee, a promise by the manufacturer that the product or service is of a certain quality. Look up information on the two types of warranties, expressed and implied. Write a paragraph comparing them.

33. **Technology** The Internet is becoming the number one source of fraudulent offers. Based on what you have learned about fraud and wise shopping, write a list of things that online shoppers should do to avoid being taken in by a fraudulent offer.

Ethical Dilemma

34. You are a new manager at a department store that sells a set of brand-name power tools for $529. For an advertised sale, the store is offering a set of its own brand of tools for $398. A customer comes in and asks for your opinion on the advertised set. You believe the advertised set is of inferior quality and its warranty provides little coverage. The regional manager is visiting your department and appears to be listening to your conversation. How do you respond to your customer?

Financial Management

Careers in Business

SUMMIT CREDIT UNION

The Summit Credit Union is a family of 20 community-based credit unions, as well as a headquarters which alone employs over 400 people. It also has an online credit union branch that is open to all who can access the Internet. Its stated mission is to improve members' financial positions.

Summit offers a variety of services and products including online banking, fee-free checking, personal and auto loans, and business services. It has 103,000 members with $1.1 billion in assets.

Member services representatives are valuable employees who provide personal account services, including cash handling and product services. A high-school diploma is required, along with good people skills and the ability to communicate effectively. Experience with handling cash is desired. Internships are made available and promotions to higher positions are preferred from within the company.

Think Critically

1. Why are member services representatives important to Summit?
2. Why do member services representatives need good people skills and the ability to communicate effectively? Why is experience in handling cash desired?

Project Objectives

- Learn about banking and credit services offered by financial institutions in your community
- Evaluate banking and credit services
- Learn about the costs of credit

©zentilia, 2009/ Used under license from Shutterstock.com

Getting Started

Read the Project Process below. Make a list of any materials you will need.

- As a class, make a list of institutions that serve your community in the categories of commercial or savings banks, savings and loans, and credit unions.

Project Process

6.1 In a group, choose one of the financial institution categories from the class list. Make a list of the services you think each financial institution in this category would offer.

6.2 Find out about banking services of local financial institutions in your category. Study the institutions' advertisements or brochures, or interview their managers. List the services offered and details about them, including interest rates, service fees, or penalties.

6.3 and 6.4 Find out about and compile a list of credit services the institutions offer. Include details such as credit terms and fees. Ask each financial institution to calculate how much it would cost in interest for one year to borrow or buy on credit something worth $5,000 for each credit option.

Chapter Review

Project Wrap-up Present the group reports on the banking and credit services of the institutions studied. After the presentations, discuss the similarities and differences among the institutions.

©Losevsky Pavel, 2009/ Used under license from Shutterstock.com

GOALS

Distinguish between deposit and nondeposit institutions

Explain the role of the Federal Reserve System

KEY TERMS

Federal Deposit Insurance Corporation (FDIC), p. 145

commercial bank, p. 145

Federal Reserve System, p. 148

JUMP START

Doing business with a financial institution is part of Brittney's money management plan. After settling into her new condo, she visited several financial institutions in her area and selected the Badger Savings Bank. She liked the convenience of the location and the friendly and helpful staff. Brittney set up her accounts so that she could do some of her banking online. She opened a personal checking account and a money market savings account. She also learned that her bank has competitive rates on certificates of deposit (CDs) and conveniently located ATMs. Is the Badger Savings Bank a deposit or a nondeposit financial institution?

Banking System

Do you think of a bank as a business? A bank is a business that sells services such as checking accounts, savings accounts, and loans in order to earn a profit. Most banks have shareholders, like other corporations. Banks get most of their income from interest they charge on loans to individuals, businesses, and governments. They also earn interest income by investing part of the money that customers deposit in savings accounts.

Banks are regulated more strictly than most other businesses. If other businesses fail, some people lose money. If a bank fails, thousands of people are potentially affected.

Banks are chartered (granted rights) by either a state or the federal government. One federal agency that regulates banks and other financial institutions is the **Federal Deposit Insurance Corporation (FDIC)**. It protects depositors' money in case of a failure of a bank or other financial institution it regulates. FDIC insurance covers all deposit accounts, including checking and savings accounts, money market accounts, and certificates of deposit. The standard insurance amount currently is $250,000 per depositor. Depositors may qualify for more coverage if they have funds in different ownership categories. Although the FDIC is a government agency, banks provide money for its operation. Almost 99 percent of all banks are FDIC members.

Some financial organizations perform some of the functions of a bank, but technically are not banks. In the business community, they may be referred to as "near-banks." Banks and near-banks can be divided into two groups: deposit institutions and nondeposit institutions.

Deposit Institutions

A *deposit institution* is one that accepts deposits from customers and provides a range of banking services. There are several kinds of deposit institutions.

Commercial Banks Many banks are commonly organized as commercial banks. A commercial bank, often called a *full-service bank*, offers a wide range of financial services that could include the following.

- Checking and savings accounts
- Loans to individuals and businesses
- International business services, including currency exchange
- Investment services, including certificates of deposit
- Safe-deposit boxes for storing valuables
- Electronic banking services, including online banking

It is becoming more common for commercial banks to have full-service branch offices in shopping centers and supermarkets. Often referred to as *financial supermarkets*, these branch offices offer everything from automated teller machines (ATMs) to loans and other personal services.

In what ways do commercial banks serve their customers?

Digital Vision/Getty Images

DID YOU KNOW ?

The first version of an ATM in the United States was installed in New York City in 1939 but was removed six months later because customers refused to use it.

COMMUNICATE

The services offered at ATMs have expanded to include the sale of train tickets, postage stamps, and shopping mall gift certificates. Some ATM users can make donations to charities and buy prepaid cell phone credits. Write a few paragraphs about what services you think ATMs will offer in the future and why consumers would want these new services. Use your imagination.

Savings and Loan Associations These associations, also known as S&Ls, traditionally specialized in offering savings accounts and making loans for home mortgages. Deregulation in the 1980s allowed these institutions to expand the array of services they could offer and become more like banks. Today, many S&Ls use the words *savings bank* in their names.

Mutual Savings Banks A *mutual savings bank* is a savings bank owned by, and operated for the benefit of, its depositors. There are no stockholders. The profits are distributed in proportion to the amount of business the participants do with the bank. While mutual savings banks provide a variety of services, they are organized mainly for savings and home loans. They are located mainly in the northeastern United States.

Credit Unions User-owned, nonprofit, cooperative financial institutions are known as *credit unions*. They are commonly formed by people in the same company, government agency, labor union, profession, church, or community. In recent years, the requirements for membership have become less restrictive. Serving members only, credit unions accept savings deposits and make loans for a variety of purposes. Credit unions also offer a wide variety of personal and business services that could include any of the following.

- Special checking accounts
- Certificates of deposit
- Electronic banking services
- Home equity loans
- Safe-deposit boxes
- Investment services
- Mortgages
- Online banking

Credit unions are regulated by the National Credit Union Association (NCUA), a federal agency similar to the FDIC. Currently, the NCUA insures depositors' funds up to $250,000 through its Insurance Fund.

Nondeposit Institutions

Nondeposit institutions are another major category of financial institutions. They are similar to banks, but they do not accept deposits. They provide a variety of financial and near-banking services as described below.

Life Insurance Companies
People often buy life insurance to provide financial security for their dependents or beneficiaries. In addition to this protection, many life insurance companies also offer investment services. Some of these investments, such as annuities and trust accounts, are sheltered from income taxes.

How can life insurance companies help you meet your financial needs?

Insurance companies often help expand business opportunities in the economy by carefully investing in new and existing companies.

Investment Companies If people want to pursue long-term growth of their money, they can buy investments through investment companies. Many investors own shares of mutual funds, which are investment funds containing a mixture of stocks and/or bonds, made available and managed by an investment company.

Consumer Finance Companies A company that specializes in making loans for long-lasting or durable goods, such as cars and appliances, and for financial emergencies is a *consumer finance company*. Because consumer finance companies specialize in making loans, they are an important part of the financial services industry. However, because the loans offered by consumer finance companies are often considered high-risk, they carry higher interest rates.

Mortgage Companies Buying a home is an important activity in our society. Mortgage companies, along with other financial institutions, provide loans for buying a home or other real estate.

Check-Cashing Outlets People who do not have bank accounts may find check-cashing outlets (CCOs) convenient for conducting financial transactions. Consumers use CCOs to cash paychecks, social security checks, and other checks. Some CCOs offer other financial services, such as electronic tax filing, money orders, private postal boxes, and utility bill payments. Services provided by CCOs are usually more expensive than those provided by other businesses.

Pawnshops Loans based on the value of tangible possessions, such as jewelry, watches, or musical instruments, are made at pawnshops. Customers are given a certain length of time to repay the loan and reclaim the property they pawned. Because they provide a service needed by consumers who are unable to get loans elsewhere, pawnshops charge higher fees than other financial institutions.

Ted's Pawn is a locally owned pawnshop in Cincinnati, Ohio. Access www.cengage.com/school/business/21biz and click on the link for Chapter 6. Browse the shop's website, and click on the *How It Works* tab. Then answer: What kinds of items do people typically pawn? According to Ohio law, what is the minimum amount of time a pawnshop must hold an item that is offered in pawn? What happens to the item if the owner does not pay off the loan at the end of the specified period?

www.cengage.com/school/business/21biz

CheckPOINT

How does a nondeposit institution differ from a deposit institution?

_____

_____

_____

The Federal Reserve System

The U.S. government set up the Federal Reserve System, often called *the Fed*, to supervise and regulate member banks and help banks serve the public efficiently. All national banks are required to join the Federal Reserve System and state banks may join. Banks that join the system are known as *member banks*. Federal Reserve Banks, part of the Federal Reserve System, serve as banks for bankers. Individuals cannot do business with them.

Structure of the Federal Reserve System

The United States is divided into 12 Federal Reserve Districts. Each district is numbered, with a central Federal Reserve Bank in each district. Some districts also have branch banks. The map below shows how the 12 districts are divided, the number assigned to each district, and the cities in which central banks and branch banks are located. A Board of Governors, located in Washington, D.C., sets policies for the Federal Reserve System.

Federal Reserve Activities

One of the important activities of the Fed is to conduct monetary policy. In doing so, the Fed can buy and sell government bonds to increase or decrease the amount of money in circulation. This helps to slow inflation if it is increasing too rapidly or to stimulate the economy if it is slowing down.

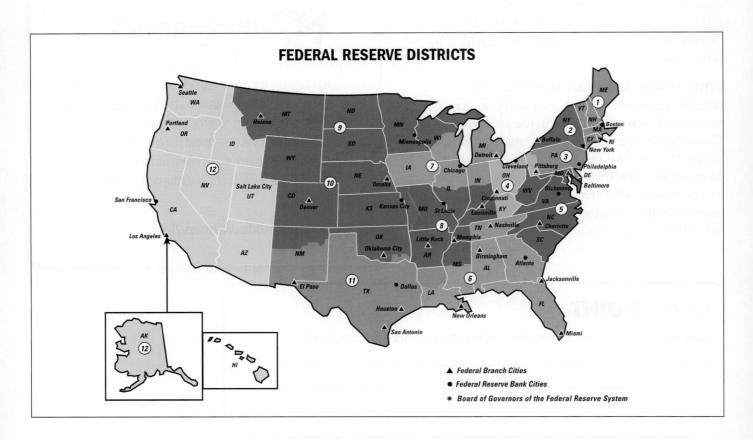

FEDERAL RESERVE DISTRICTS

▲ Federal Branch Cities
● Federal Reserve Bank Cities
✳ Board of Governors of the Federal Reserve System

Consumers go to their banks to deposit money or to get a loan. The Federal Reserve Bank serves its member banks by accepting deposits and providing services, including lending the banks money. Interest that the Fed charges member banks on money borrowed is called the *discount rate*. The interest rate that the Fed charges member banks affects the interest rate that banks charge for money they lend out. The interest rate member banks pay to the Fed is added to the interest they charge consumers to earn a profit.

Another service provided by the Fed is the holding of reserves. Banks cannot lend out all of their customers' deposits. The Fed requires banks to keep a certain amount of customers' money on deposit with a Federal Reserve Bank in case the banks' customers need to withdraw more funds. As a result, a bank lends only a certain percentage of deposited funds and keeps the rest in reserve. This regulation helps the banking system and the economy operate efficiently, and it protects deposits.

Here is how the reserve requirement works: If a customer deposits $1,000 and the bank must hold 15 percent of deposits in reserve, $150 is held back and $850 can be loaned out.

$1,000 \times 0.15 = $150
$1,000 - $150 = $850

Another service of the Fed is clearing checks for member banks. *Clearing* refers to the paying of checks among different banks in different locations. The Fed processes millions of checks each day to make sure that the correct amounts are added to and subtracted from the appropriate accounts.

Photodisc/Getty Images

Why are reserve requirements necessary?

TEAMWORK

Locate your Federal Reserve District. Work in groups to learn as much as possible about your district. Talk with local bankers about relations with their central bank. Get information from the Internet and other sources. Write a report and make a group presentation to the class.

CheckPOINT

What is the main purpose of the Federal Reserve System?

_____

_____

_____

Think Critically

1. Why is it necessary to have the FDIC and NCUA insure bank deposits?

_____

_____

_____

2. Do you think consumers would be better off if there were just one kind of bank in the economy? Why or why not?

_____

_____

_____

_____

3. In what ways is the Federal Reserve System important to you as a customer of your local bank?

_____

_____

_____

_____

4. Do you think that the Fed should allow a bank to lend all of its deposits out so that it can make more money? Why or why not?

_____

_____

_____

_____

Make Academic Connections

5. **Advertising** Look at a local newspaper that contains several advertisements by banks and near-banks. Write a one-page report summarizing the ads. Note differences in services, interest rates, and other features.

6. **Consumer Economics** Which of a commercial bank's financial services are important to you now? Which will be important to you in the future?

_____

_____

_____

_____

JUMP START

Emilio received a refund check from a business in another state. He endorsed the check and deposited it in his checking account. A few days later, the bank informed him that the account on which the check had been drawn was closed. The check bounced, and the amount of the check plus a fee was deducted from Emilio's account. He contacted the business to straighten out the problem. In another incident, Emilio encountered a problem when he mailed a check to a business as payment for an online order and the check got lost. He had to contact his bank, issue a stop payment order, and then write a new check to replace the first one. The bank charged him for the stop payment order. In both instances, Emilio acted responsibly. Why did he have to pay the fees?

©Jason Stitt, 2009/ Used under license from Shutterstock.com

GOALS

Explain the use of checks and other payment methods

Describe the financial services used by consumers

KEY TERMS

money order, p. 153

electronic funds transfer (EFT), p. 154

interest, p. 155

Checks and Other Payment Methods

Businesses generally accept cash from consumers as payment for goods and services. Consumers often prefer to use other means of payment. They may find checks and debit cards more convenient and safer than carrying cash. Electronic funds transfers (EFTs) are also becoming increasingly popular as a means of payment by businesses and consumers.

Checks

Many people open checking accounts with a bank or other financial institution, enabling them to write checks to make payments. There are basic requirements for a check transaction to be legal. The following illustration shows important parts of a legal check.

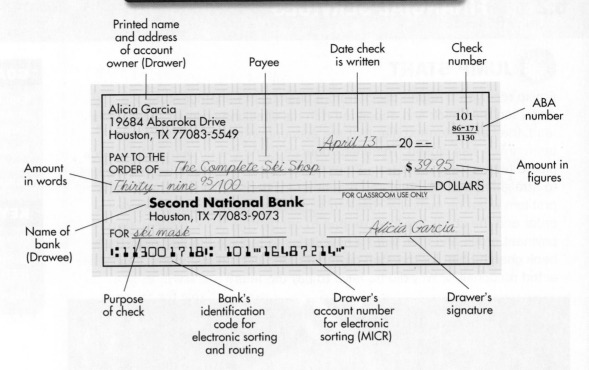

Printed name and address of account owner (Drawer)

Payee

Date check is written

Check number

ABA number

Amount in words

Amount in figures

Name of bank (Drawee)

Purpose of check

Bank's identification code for electronic sorting and routing

Drawer's account number for electronic sorting (MICR)

Drawer's signature

Alicia Garcia
19684 Absaroka Drive
Houston, TX 77083-5549

101
86-171
1130

April 13   20 — —

PAY TO THE
ORDER OF   *The Complete Ski Shop* $ *39.95*

Thirty - nine ⁹⁵/₁₀₀   DOLLARS

FOR CLASSROOM USE ONLY

Second National Bank
Houston, TX 77083-9073

FOR *ski mask*   *Alicia Garcia*

⑈⑈3001718⑈ 101 ⑈1648 7214⑈

Writing a Check Although checks are less commonly used these days, it is important for you to know how to write one properly when you do. There are three parties involved in every check: the drawer, the payee, and the drawee. The *drawer* is the owner of the checking account and the person who signs the check. The *payee* is the person to whom the check is written. The *drawee* is the bank or other financial institution that pays the amount of the check.

Poor check writing can cause problems and financial difficulties. Write checks only on forms provided by your bank. Write checks in ink, and don't let anyone change what you have written.

Before writing a check, it is important to record the transaction, including the date, the payee, and the amount of the check. This can be done on a check stub, which is attached to the check, or in a separate check register provided with the checks. Then, follow these seven steps when writing a check.

1. Write checks in order by check number.

2. Write the date in the proper space on the check.

3. Write the payee's name on the line following "Pay to the order of."

4. Write the amount of the check in figures after the printed dollar sign.

5. Write the amount of dollars in words on the line below the payee's name.

6. Write the purpose of the payment on the line following "For" at the bottom of the check.

7. Sign the bottom of your checks with the same signature that you wrote on the signature card when you opened your checking account.

When writing checks, be sure that the amounts written in figures and words agree and that your checking account balance is sufficient for the bank to pay the amount of the check. Avoid making the check payable to "cash" because that allows anyone to cash the check if it is lost.

Stopping Payment   In certain situations, you may want to instruct your bank not to pay a check that you have written. To do so, your bank will ask you to fill out a *stop payment order*, which is a written notice from the drawer telling the bank not to pay a certain check. This order includes the date, check number, amount, payee, and the drawer's signature.

Banks charge a high fee for stopping payment on a check, so stop a payment only for a good reason. If you believe that a check you have written has been lost in the mail or has been stolen, file a stop payment order on the one that was lost or stolen before you write the new check.

Accepting and Cashing Checks   Your responsibility as an endorser (the person who signs the check) or drawer of checks is very important. As the endorser, you are guaranteeing that the amount on the check will be paid. If a check you write or endorse turns out to be bad, you are liable for the amount of the check.

According to law, a check is payable on demand. This means that it is payable when the holder of the check presents it to the drawer's bank for payment. A bank may refuse to accept a check if it is presented for payment too long after the date on which it was written. Some checks have a 60-day limit. Usually, you will have no trouble cashing a check where you are known or can prove your identity. However, legally no person or business has to accept a check as a form of payment.

Other Payment Methods

In addition to checks, there are several other payment methods. These include money orders, certified checks, cashier's checks, and electronic funds transfer.

Money Orders   A money order is a form of payment that orders the issuing agency to pay the amount printed on the form to a specified payee. The amount paid for the money order covers the amount of the money order plus a fee. There are four types of money orders.

- *Bank Money Order*   If you do not have a checking account at a bank, a bank money order may be useful. Bank money orders sold by banks state the amount of money to be paid to the person or business named on the form. The amount is on deposit in the bank, thus assuring payment.

- *Postal Money Order*   You may purchase a postal money order from the U.S. Postal Service. It contains the payee's name, your name and address, and the purpose of the money order and can be cashed only after it is signed by the payee. These are often used because they are safer to mail, since you can make a claim to the post office using your receipt if the money order is lost or stolen. The amount to be paid is on deposit with the U.S. Postal Service.

DID YOU KNOW ?

You can use bank money orders to send payments to other countries in the currency of those countries.

- *Express Money Order* This type of money order is issued by various organizations, including supermarkets, pharmacies, and convenience stores.
- *Telegraphic Money Order* This type of money order directs another telegraph office to pay a sum of money to a certain person or business. The amount of the money order is deposited with the sending office. These are used mainly in an emergency when money must be delivered quickly.

Certified Checks A certified check is a personal check for which a bank has guaranteed payment. A bank officer will immediately deduct the amount of the check from your checking account, stamp the certification on the face of the check, and sign or initial it. You will have to pay a small fee for this service.

Cashier's Checks A cashier's check is a check that a bank draws on its own funds. It costs the amount of the check plus a service fee. After receiving payment, a bank officer makes out the check to the payee you specify. Cashier's checks are more acceptable than personal checks from unknown individuals.

Electronic Funds Transfer The use of computers and other technology to move funds electronically from one account to another is known as **electronic funds transfer (EFT)**. This aspect of electronic banking includes the use of automated teller machines (ATMs), debit cards, point-of-sale transactions, direct deposits, and automatic bill payments.

Monthly bills, such as utility bills, can be paid automatically each month by authorizing your bank to transfer the money electronically from your account to the designated company.

In point-of-sale transactions, businesses accept debit cards to pay for purchases. Some checks can also be point-of-sale transactions if the business has the technology to convert the check into an electronic money transfer. Direct deposits are made when your paycheck or other payments are automatically deposited to your checking or savings accounts.

Digital Vision/Getty Images

Why are EFTs a popular way to make payments?

CheckPOINT

Why is there a need for other payment methods besides checks?

_____

_____

Types of Financial Services

Common financial services available to consumers include saving services, payment services, lending services, storage services, financial and investment services, and trust management services.

Saving Services

One of the main services that financial institutions offer is accepting money from customers for safe-keeping. Money deposited in a savings account not only provides security, it also allows you to earn interest on the money on deposit. Interest is the amount banks pay you for the use of your money. Banks hold some of the money on deposit in reserve and lend out or invest the remainder.

Payment Services

The ability to transfer money to others is necessary for daily business activities. Types of payment services include checking accounts, debit cards, online payments, and automatic withdrawals.

Lending Services

Banks make loans because most of their income is from interest they charge borrowers. Just as banks pay you interest for the use of the money you deposit in your savings accounts, you must pay banks interest for the use of the money they lend you. When you apply for a loan, your credit report will be a major factor in deciding whether or not the loan will be granted.

Banks offer many types of lending services. These include auto loans, business loans, and home mortgages. Banks may also issue credit cards. When you use a bank credit card, you are essentially borrowing money from the bank to pay for your purchases.

Tech Literacy

SMART CARD TECHNOLOGY

Smart cards are described as minicomputers—without screens or keyboards—that can store and process thousands of bytes of electronic data. A smart card the size of a credit card can allow you to shop and make cash or credit purchases. You can store data about financial and personal matters, your driver's license and auto insurance, medical insurance coverage, and employment information and have it with you at all times. Items can be purchased with just a swipe of the card. With certain cards, when you return home, you can display records of all your spending on your home computer and print records if needed.

THINK CRITICALLY

What are the advantages and disadvantages of having a smart card?

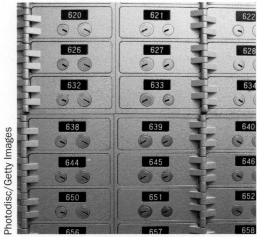
What kind of items would you store in a safe-deposit box?

Storage Services

Banks offer *safe-deposit boxes*, a secure place where you can store valuables. Safe-deposit boxes are in well-guarded vaults and are the safest places in which to keep valuables such as jewelry, bond and stock certificates, and legal records. These boxes are rented for a nominal fee. The box can be opened only by the renter of the box or someone who has been given the right to open the box by the renter. To gain access, you must sign in and have your signature compared with the one you wrote when you rented your safe-deposit box or provide a special code.

Financial and Investment Services

Most banks offer advice on investments. *Investments* are savings put to work to earn money, such as savings or money market accounts that earn interest. Banks also sell federal government bonds and certificates of deposit. *Certificates of deposit (CDs)* are a special kind of savings account that requires deposits to be kept in the bank for a specified period of time. CDs pay higher interest rates than regular savings accounts. Many banks also provide advice on stocks, bonds, and mutual funds available in the securities markets.

Trust Management Services

A *trust* is a legal arrangement in which money or other property is turned over to the financial institution for safekeeping and to be managed for a purpose stated in the trust. Financial institutions that specialize in the handling of trusts are called *trust companies*. Trusts are used by people of all ages. They are especially useful for young people and for some elderly people. A young person who inherits money may not have the skill and experience to manage it wisely. Elderly people who are ill may use a trust to help manage their money. Trust officers make investments on behalf of the trust owners and inform them of the status of their trusts.

TEAMWORK

Divide into six groups—one group for each of the six types of financial services offered by financial institutions. Find out what local banks offer in the service category chosen by your group. Write a report and make a presentation to the class for discussion.

CheckPOINT

Why are saving services important to consumers and banks?

_____

_____

Think Critically

1. What is the advantage of a check over a money order for the person who writes the check? What is the advantage of a money order over a check for the person who receives the money order?

_____

_____

_____

2. Why do you think people and businesses are not legally required to accept a check for payment?

_____

_____

_____

3. Describe a scenario, other than the one described in this lesson, in which you would want to stop a check.

_____

_____

_____

Make Academic Connections

4. **Business Law** "Legal tender" is a basic principle in business law. Look up the definition of legal tender and find out some of the aspects of this principle. How does this principle apply to the offering of a check versus a cash payment? What other forms of payment are affected?

_____

_____

_____

_____

5. **Marketing** Contact a local bank and obtain information on safe-deposit boxes. Record the different sizes of boxes available, the cost of renting each size, and procedures for gaining access to a safe-deposit box. Create a spreadsheet for that institution's safe-deposit boxes. Include box sizes, costs, and access procedures.

6. **Research** In addition to certified checks and cashier's checks, you may someday find the need for traveler's checks. Research traveler's checks to learn more about them. Discuss situations in which these kinds of checks might be used.

JUMP START

Brianna is a typical U.S. consumer, using credit for many purposes—to buy a car, pay medical bills, and take vacations. She also uses credit for its convenience when making smaller purchases, such as meals, gas, and clothing. When she travels on business, she uses the Triad Bakery's company credit card. The company also secures long-term loans to buy property and equipment and short-term loans to meet temporary needs for cash. What should Brianna and the bakery keep in mind to ensure they use credit wisely?

©Andresr, 2009/ Used under license from Shutterstock.com

Credit in the Economy

Individuals, businesses, and governments have something in common—they all have needs and wants, but not enough money to satisfy them. Using credit to satisfy needs and wants is a basic part of the U.S. economy. Many consumers could not buy new cars, furniture, or large appliances without using credit. Governments could not finance the building of roads and schools without borrowing money. Retail stores could not offer as wide a variety of merchandise if they had to pay for it before it was sold.

What Is Credit?

Credit is the privilege of using someone else's money for a period of time. That privilege is based on the belief that the person receiving credit will honor a promise to repay the amount owed at a future date. The credit transaction creates a debtor and a creditor. The **debtor** is anyone who buys on credit or receives a loan. A **creditor** is the one who sells on credit or who grants a loan.

The credit system uses forms and legal documents to make the credit transaction sound and understood by all parties. A credit or loan agreement is an enforceable contract. The credit system also depends on trust between the debtor and creditor. This trust means that the creditor believes the debtor will honor his or her promise to pay later for goods and services received and used. The credit system could not operate without trust.

With credit card transactions, there is a legal assumption that the amount borrowed will be repaid. It is part of the agreement you sign when your credit card is issued. However, if you borrow a large amount of money or make a large credit purchase from a store, you usually will be asked to sign a written agreement stating that you will pay your debt in a certain period of time. A credit agreement means that the debtor promises to pay and the creditor trusts that the debtor will pay the amount owed.

Types of Credit

When you borrow money to be used for some special purpose, you are using *loan credit*. There are several types of loans available from banks, credit unions, savings and loan associations, and consumer finance companies. Loan credit usually involves a written contract. The debtor often agrees to repay the loan in specified amounts, called *installments*, over a period of time. Installment loans often are used for the purchase of large appliances and furniture.

If you charge a purchase at the time you buy the good or service, you are using *sales credit*. Sales credit is offered by most retail and wholesale businesses. It involves customers using charge accounts and credit cards.

When a business receives goods from a wholesaler and pays for them over a specified period of time, the business is using *trade credit*. Trade credit terms are stated as, for example, "2/10, n/30." This means that the business can take a 2 percent discount if the bill is paid within 10 days from the billing date, and the full amount, or net, must be paid within 30 days. With those terms, a business that owes $5,000 will save $100 by paying within 10 days ($5,000 × 0.02 = $100). Businesses may obtain short-term loans to pay bills or long-term loans to buy land, equipment, and buildings.

Granting of Credit

You have learned that trust between the debtor and creditor is essential if credit is to be granted. Standard business procedures require you to show that you are a good credit risk before credit will be extended to you. Not everyone who desires credit will receive it.

Credit Applications When you apply for credit or a loan, the lender will ask you to fill out an application. A *credit application* is a form on which you provide information needed by a lender to make a decision about granting credit. Some companies accept credit applications online.

An important part of a credit application is credit references. A *credit reference* is a business or individual from whom you have received credit in the past and who is able and willing to provide information about your creditworthiness—whether you pay your bills on time. The financial

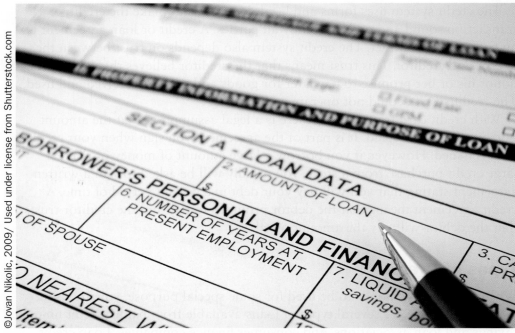

What kinds of information might be requested on a credit application?

information you provide and information received from your credit references help a business decide whether or not to extend loan or sales credit to you.

The following questions can be asked of all individuals requesting credit: How much do you earn? What other debts do you have? How long have you worked for your present employer? What property do you own? Important decisions cannot be made without accurate answers to these questions.

The Three Cs of Credit When deciding whether or not to grant credit, businesses consider three main factors: character, capacity, and capital.

- *Character* refers to your honesty and willingness to pay a debt when it is due. It is your history of paying bills on time, showing creditors that you are a good credit risk.

- *Capacity* refers to your ability to pay a debt when it is due, and whether you have enough income to pay your bills. This compares your level of income to the amount of debt to be incurred.

- *Capital* is the value of the borrower's possessions, including money and property owned. Capital may include a car that is paid for and a house on which a large amount has been paid. The amount of capital you have gives the lender some assurance of your ability to repay your loan.

CheckPOINT

Write a brief definition of debtor and creditor.

_____

_____

Benefits and Concerns of Credit

Both businesses and individuals benefit from the use of credit. But credit can also create financial problems. Because you are spending income you have not yet earned or received, consumers and businesses must use it carefully.

Benefits of Credit

Businesses benefit in several ways. Customers who buy on credit tend to purchase more, and the business then earns increased profits. If the business buys its merchandise using trade credit, the merchandise can be paid for after the business has received income from the sale of the merchandise.

Consumers also receive benefits from the wise use of credit, including

- *Convenience* Credit can make it convenient for you to shop without carrying a lot of cash.
- *Immediate possession* Credit allows you to have the item you want right away without waiting until you can save up enough money to buy it.
- *Savings* With credit you can buy an item when it goes on sale, often at a lower price. Stores often send special sales notices to credit customers.
- *Credit rating* If you buy on credit and pay your bills on time, you gain a reputation for being dependable and establish a good credit rating. That will help you get loans or other credit when needed in the future.
- *Useful in emergencies* Access to credit can help you in an emergency. If you are away from home and out of cash and have a crisis, a credit card could come to your rescue. If you are between jobs and have a good credit rating, credit might help you pay bills when your income level is low.

Cross-Cultural Relationships

CREDIT CARDS IN MALAYSIA

In Islamic finance, there is no such thing as a loan. Yet there is a movement underway to make credit cards available to consumers in Malaysia, a country whose official religion is Islam. In a recent year, the Islamic credit card market (which is concentrated in the Middle East, southeast Asia, and northern Africa) had more than 250 million customers. Banks, both Islamic and conventional, are investing in credit card structures, cards that are interest-free and are Shariah-compliant (meet Islamic standards).

A limited number of credit cards have been issued, and it is anticipated that a battle of Islamic credit cards will occur as more and more issuers, including MasterCard and Visa, enter the marketplace.

Think Critically

What advice would you give to Malaysian consumers when they receive their credit cards and start using them?

What could happen if credit isn't used wisely?

Concerns of Credit

Buying on credit is convenient and can be beneficial. However, there are some concerns about using credit if you are not careful about how you use it. Those concerns include the following.

- *Overbuying* This is the most common concern of credit buying. Resist buying things that are more expensive than you can afford or buying attractive items that you do not really need.

- *Careless buying* It is important to continue to check advertisements, make comparisons, and buy at the right place or time. Because credit is convenient, it is tempting to buy now rather than wait for a better price.

- *Higher prices* You can expect higher prices in businesses where credit is offered. Extending credit is expensive and requires good record keeping for credit sales and payments. Increased business costs are passed along to customers. Businesses that accept only cash can sell items at lower prices.

- *Overuse of credit* Buying now and paying later might sound like a good idea, but if too many payments must be made later, the total of those payments could be a problem. It is important to keep a record of the total amount of all money owed so that it does not exceed your ability to pay.

Businesses and governments can also get into credit trouble. Too much debt can lead some companies into bankruptcy when creditors force them to make payments. We all need to manage credit properly.

TEAMWORK

Overuse of credit can lead to bankruptcy. Working in groups, use the Internet and other sources of information to learn more about personal bankruptcy. Discuss the costs, procedures, and requirements for filing for bankruptcy. In addition, discuss its advantages and disadvantages. Compile a report summarizing your group's findings.

CheckPOINT

How can credit lead to careless buying?

_____

_____

Think Critically

1. Explain why trust is an important factor in granting credit.

_____

_____

_____

2. Explain how trade credit benefits both wholesalers and retailers.

_____

_____

_____

3. Describe a strategy for using credit wisely. What kinds of items would you buy on credit? What kinds of items would you pay for with cash? Why?

_____

_____

_____

Make Academic Connections

4. **Business Math** Two businesses have trade credit offered to them. Company A always takes advantage of the discount. Company B never does. With the data provided below, compute how much Company A saves over Company B.

Invoice Amount	Trade Credit Terms	Amount Saved by Company A
$395	1/15, n/30	_____
$1,050	2/10, n/20	_____
$5,740	3/15, n/90	_____
$10,000	2/20, n/60	_____
$30,800	1/10, n/30	_____
$13,500	3/15, n/90	_____
	Total	_____

5. **Communication** Obtain a copy of a loan application or credit card application. Read through it carefully to analyze the kinds of questions included. Make a list of those questions. Write a statement explaining the ways in which you think each question is important to the creditor. Include a summary statement about why it is important to answer all of the questions and to be truthful in answering them.

GOALS

Explain why interest and finance charges are part of the cost of credit

Describe six laws that regulate credit

KEY TERMS

finance charge, p. 166

annual percentage rate (APR), p. 166

 JUMP START

Emilio had a serious problem. While he was working out at the health club, someone broke into his locker and stole his wallet. It was recovered, but his money, bank credit card, gas credit card, department store charge card, and driver's license were all missing. He kept a file folder in which he had his credit card numbers and immediately called the bank, the gas company, and the department store to report the theft. He drove to the Department of Transportation office and applied for a replacement license. Because he reported the theft of his credit cards promptly, he did not incur any financial loss for charges the thief made to his accounts. What might have happened if Emilio had not known about the laws regarding lost credit cards?

©Monkey Business Images, 2009/ Used under license from Shutterstock.com

The Cost of Credit

Consumer credit enables you to have and enjoy goods and services now and to pay for them later. Always remember, though, that credit is not free. The costs associated with credit must be paid by those who use it. One of the basic costs is the interest that you pay on money borrowed. The three factors involved in calculating the cost of the interest to be paid on a loan or charge account are

1. *Principal*   The amount of the loan
2. *Interest rate*   The percent of interest that is charged and applied to your loan, expressed as a fraction or decimal
3. *Time*   The length of time for which interest will be charged, in years

Simple Interest

On single-payment loans where the amount borrowed is repaid in one lump sum, interest is often expressed as simple interest. Simple interest is based on time in years. The formula for computing simple interest is

Interest = Principal × Rate × Time

For example, if $1,000 is borrowed at 9 percent for one year, the amount of interest would be calculated as shown below.

Interest = $1,000 × 0.09 × 1 = $90

In calculating interest, you need to remember that the interest rate must be expressed in the form of a fraction or a decimal. Also remember that interest is charged for each dollar or part of a dollar borrowed.

For simple interest, the interest rate is based on a one-year period of time. If the actual period of time is more than or less than one year, the calculation of interest must be adjusted. For example, the amount of interest would be double ($180) if the loan were for 2 years.

$1,000 × 0.09 × 2 = $180

The amount of interest would be one-half ($45) if the loan were for only six months. Remember that six months is one-half, or 0.5, year.

$1,000 × 0.09 × 0.5 = $45

Installment Interest

When borrowing money, several payments are usually made instead of one large single payment. Loans that are repaid in partial payments are called installment (or consumer) loans. Each payment is called an installment. With an installment loan, the borrower is often given a payment schedule to show the amount due each month. Installment loans may entail paying the same amount each month or paying decreasing payments as the loan amount decreases.

Business Math Connection

Calculate the amount of interest that would be charged for each loan.

A. $10,000 borrowed at 7 percent interest for 1 year
B. $500 borrowed at 12 percent interest for 3 months
C. $25,000 borrowed at 6 percent interest for 4 years

SOLUTION
The formula for calculating simple interest is

Interest = Principal × Rate × Time

A. $10,000 × 0.07 × 1 = $700 interest
B. 3 months is 3/12 year, or 0.25, so $500 × 0.12 × 0.25 = $15 interest
C. $25,000 × 0.06 × 4 = $6,000 interest

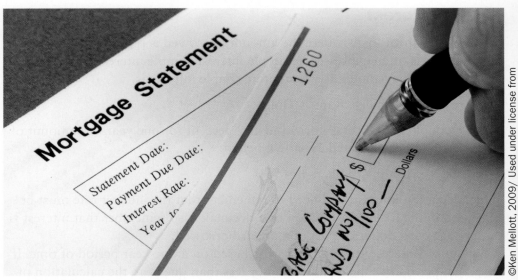

What is an installment loan?

With some loans, the amount of the interest is added to the amount borrowed, the principal, and is paid as part of the equal monthly installments. On other loans, the amount of interest is calculated on the amount that is unpaid at the end of each month. Then, the monthly payment is applied to both the principal and the interest, with a larger percentage applied to the interest for the first payments. Near the end of the loan, after much of the interest has been paid, more of the monthly payment is applied to the principal.

Finance Charges and APR

When borrowing money or charging a purchase, you should consider the finance charge and the annual percentage rate (APR). Federal law requires that lenders disclose the finance charge and APR in all credit agreements, whether for sales or loan credit. The **finance charge** is the total *dollar* cost of credit. Interest is not the only cost included in the finance charge. Other charges include service fees for the time and money it takes a creditor to investigate your credit history, process your credit application, and keep records of your payments and balances. Lenders may also charge for credit insurance, which repays the balance of the amount owed if the borrower dies or becomes disabled.

The **annual percentage rate (APR)** is the *percentage* cost of credit stated on a yearly basis. The APR makes it easier to compare costs of credit from various lenders.

CheckPOINT

What is the formula for computing simple interest?

_____

_____

The Regulation of Credit

Federal and state laws have been passed to protect consumers who engage in credit transactions. Although most companies are honest in their business dealings, some are not. The Truth in Lending Act of 1968 was the first in a series of credit protection laws that deal with various aspects of credit and lending practices. Each law was intended to remove some of the problems and confusion surrounding the use of credit.

Truth in Lending Act

Under the provisions of the *Truth in Lending Act*, you must be told the cost of credit before you sign a credit agreement. The law requires the lender to clearly state the annual percentage rate (APR) and the total finance charge.

This law also protects you against unauthorized use of credit by limiting your liability for unauthorized credit card purchases if your card is lost or stolen. The law limits your liability to $50 for unauthorized credit purchases made prior to notifying the card issuer. You are not liable for any fraudulent charges made after you have notified the credit card company. You can notify the company by telephone, but you should also put your notification in writing.

In addition, this act requires a grace period of three business days in which purchasers can change their mind about a credit agreement that is made in their home or in a place that is not the seller's permanent place of business. For example, this would apply to door-to-door sales. This three-day period is referred to as a *cooling-off period*.

Before signing a credit agreement, what information should you be given as required by law?

©Andresr, 2009/ Used under license from Shutterstock.com

Equal Credit Opportunity Act

The *Equal Credit Opportunity Act* prohibits creditors from denying credit because of age, race, sex, or marital status. It aims to prevent discrimination in granting credit. Young people who have entered the labor market cannot be denied credit based on their age alone. Older, possibly retired, people also have protection under this act. A married woman who previously found it difficult to establish credit in her own name now has a legal right to do so if she proves her creditworthiness. Upon request, a creditor must give a written statement of the reasons for rejection to any person who has been denied credit.

Fair Credit Billing Act

The *Fair Credit Billing Act* requires prompt correction of billing mistakes when they are brought to the attention of a business in a specific manner. To get a correction of an error, you must notify your creditor within 60 days after the date on which your credit statement was mailed. It is best to report errors as soon as you find them. Your notification must be specific in describing the problem. Provisions of this law include the following.

- While waiting for an answer to your complaint, you are not required to pay any amount in question.

- The creditor must acknowledge your complaint within 30 days unless the matter is corrected before then.

- You do not pay finance charges on any amount in error.

- If no error is found, the creditor must bill you again and may include finance charges that have accumulated plus any minimum payments that were missed during this time.

- You may withhold payment of any balance due on defective merchandise or services purchased with a credit card.

Why is it important to check your credit card statement closely each month?

In each instance above, the law presumes that you have acted responsibly. It protects you if you have made a good faith effort to work with the business.

Fair Credit Reporting Act

The *Fair Credit Reporting Act* gives consumers the right to know what specific information credit bureaus are providing to potential creditors, employers, and insurers. This law states that if you are denied credit based on information contained in a credit bureau's report, you must be given the name, address, and phone number of that credit bureau.

Before this law was enacted, many consumers were unaware that reports on their credit and bill-paying transactions were available to potential lenders and also to prospective employers. This act makes those reports available to consumers so that they can review this information. It also provides ways to correct errors. Consumers have the right to have inaccurate information investigated, corrected, and deleted from their credit record. Any information dealing with personal bankruptcy that is more than ten years old must also be deleted from the record. Other adverse information must be deleted if it is more than seven years old.

Consumer Credit Reporting Reform Act

The *Consumer Credit Reporting Reform Act*, which amended the Fair Credit Reporting Act, increases consumer protection against unfair, adverse decisions based on credit reports. An unfavorable credit report can cause consumers to pay higher interest rates on a loan or to be denied a loan.

This act establishes stronger regulations of credit reporting agencies in order to minimize the reporting of false and inaccurate information. Creditors must certify that disputed data is accurate, and if it is incorrect, the consumer can sue for damages. The federal government and state attorneys general can also sue creditors for civil damages.

In addition, this act requires employers to inform applicants or employees in advance if credit reports will be obtained for use in employment decisions.

Fair Debt Collection Practices Act

A debt collection agency may contact people whose credit payments are overdue. To prevent threats and other inappropriate actions, the *Fair Debt Collections Act* requires that debt collectors treat individuals fairly. It bans poor collection activities but does not eliminate debts that are owed.

©Sean Prior, 2009/ Used under license from Shutterstock.com

Why was the Fair Debt Collection Practices Act passed?

A debt collector may contact individuals in person or by mail, telephone, telegram, or fax. A debt collector may not make contact at a place or time that is normally inconvenient such as before 8 a.m. or after 9 p.m. Collectors also may not make contact at a person's place of work if the employer prohibits such contact.

Build a Good Credit Rating

Building your own good credit rating is important. There are many ways to do this. Establishing a good employment record while working part-time jobs can be helpful. Making regular deposits to your savings account tells others that you have good money management habits and could be a good credit risk. Some people establish credit records by making small purchases on credit and making payments according to the terms laid out by their creditors.

How can a good employment record help you build a good credit rating?

If a consumer gets into a situation where payments cannot be made as agreed, the consumer should contact the creditor. Often a plan can be worked out where payments are reduced in size and the debt paid off over a longer time period. This plan is referred to as a *debt repayment plan* and benefits both the debtor and the creditor.

If necessary, special help is also available. Credit counseling is available in many communities. A *credit counselor* can suggest actions that can be taken to reduce spending and eliminate difficulties with credit. The National Foundation of Consumer Credit is a nonprofit organization that can direct consumers to local credit assistance programs. There are hundreds of member organizations, known as Consumer Credit Counseling Services (CCCS), that operate local offices around the country. Consumers should be cautious of for-profit credit counseling services.

CheckPOINT

Why is there a need for credit protection laws?

_____

_____

Think Critically

1. Why should you have to pay interest on money you borrow through a loan or a credit purchase?

_____

_____

_____

2. In what ways is the APR useful to consumers who need to borrow money or buy something on installment credit?

_____

_____

_____

3. Describe a scenario in which you would need to use the Fair Credit Billing Act to protect your credit rating.

_____

_____

_____

Make Academic Connections

4. **Business Math** Allison needs $5,000 for a major purchase. After shopping around, she has found that there are some important differences in the amount of interest different lenders charge. Compute the total amount, including simple interest, that she would pay on each of the loans described below. Calculate the difference between the highest cost and lowest cost loan.

   Loan A   5% interest rate, payment due in three years   _____

   Loan B   9% interest rate, payment due in two years   _____

   Loan C   14% interest rate, payment due in one year   _____

   Difference between highest cost and lowest cost loan   _____

5. **Advertising** Credit repair companies may offer a quick fix for credit problems in return for high fees. Find and analyze an advertisement for a credit repair company. Write a one-page summary of your analysis of the company's statements in the advertisement. Include advice you would give someone who is considering using this credit repair company.

6. **Communication** Write an article for your school or local newspaper reporting how federal laws and regulations relating to credit protect consumers. Include statements about why these laws are necessary and why consumers should be knowledgeable about their rights under these laws.

Chapter Summary

6.1 **Financial Institutions**
- A. Banks and near-banks can be deposit or nondeposit institutions.
- B. The Federal Reserve System helps member banks serve the public.

6.2 **Financial Services**
- A. Consumers may use checks and other payment methods to purchase goods and services.
- B. Common financial services include accepting deposits, making payments, giving loans, storing valuables, giving financial and investment advice, and managing trusts.

6.3 **Credit Basics**
- A. Credit is the use of someone else's money and is granted based on the three Cs, which are character, capacity, and capital.
- B. Although there are many benefits to credit, consumers must take precautions to avoid credit problems.

6.4 **Credit Costs and Laws**
- A. A finance charge is the cost of credit stated as a dollar amount. The APR is the cost of credit stated as a percentage, making it easier to compare costs of credit among lenders.
- B. Credit is regulated by the Truth in Lending Act, Equal Credit Opportunity Act, Fair Credit Billing Act, Fair Credit Reporting Act, Consumer Credit Reporting Reform Act, and Fair Debt Collection Practices Act.

Vocabulary Builder

Choose the term that best fits the definition. Write the letter of the answer in the space provided. Some terms may not be used.

_____ 1. System organized to supervise and regulate member banks and help them serve the public efficiently

_____ 2. Use of computers and other technology to move funds electronically from one account to another

_____ 3. Privilege of using someone else's money for a period of time

_____ 4. Protects depositors' money in case of a failure of a bank or other financial institution

_____ 5. One who sells on credit or who grants a loan

_____ 6. Amount banks pay you for the use of your money

_____ 7. Full-service bank that offers a wide range of financial services

_____ 8. The percentage cost of credit stated on a yearly basis

_____ 9. Anyone who buys on credit or receives a loan

_____10. Form of payment that orders the issuing agency to pay the amount printed on the form to a specified payee

a. annual percentage rate (APR)

b. commercial bank

c. credit

d. creditor

e. debtor

f. electronic funds transfer (EFT)

g. Federal Deposit Insurance Corporation (FDIC)

h. Federal Reserve System

i. finance charge

j. interest

k. money order

Review Concepts

www.cengage.com/
school/business/21biz

Point Your Browser

11. Name six services offered by a full-service bank.

12. What is a mutual savings bank?

13. Name eight services credit unions offer.

14. What are six kinds of nondeposit institutions?

15. What is the discount rate?

16. What are the three parties to a check?

17. When should a stop payment order be filed with a bank?

18. Describe "interest" in terms of saving money and borrowing money.

19. What are some uses for safe-deposit boxes?

20. What are the three Cs of credit?

_____

_____

21. Define each of the elements in the formula for computing simple interest.

_____

_____

_____

22. Name two types of credit and describe each.

_____

_____

Apply What You Learned

23. Why should the amount of a check be written both in figures and in words? Which amount would you assume is correct if they do not agree?

_____

_____

_____

24. Why have banks begun to open branches that offer a variety of banking services in shopping centers and supermarkets?

_____

_____

_____

25. When do banks find it necessary to borrow money from a Federal Reserve Bank?

_____

_____

_____

26. Why are interest rates on credit card balances so much higher than interest rates on other loans?

_____

_____

_____

27. Why is it necessary for a bank to charge fees for stop payment orders and for bad checks that were deposited?

_____

_____

_____

28. Why might lenders refuse to give credit to someone based on his or her age, sex, race, or marital status? Give at least one reason in each of these discrimination categories.

_____

_____

29. Why is there a 60-day limit during which you must notify a creditor if you believe there is an error in your bill?

_____

_____

30. Why is it important for consumers to be able to review their credit report?

_____

_____

Make Academic Connections

31. **Economics** Contact one or more banks that serve your community and find out what kind of local or area investments they have made. Write a paragraph describing those investments and how they have benefited your community.

32. **Art** Make a poster showing what consumers should consider when selecting a financial institution. Illustrate each of the points with pictures or drawings. Include a sentence about why each point is important.

33. **Communication** Consider several individuals you know who could be a credit reference for you. Write a letter asking permission to use their names as a credit reference. Include in your letter the type of loan or credit you will be seeking and why you believe you are a good credit risk.

Ethical Dilemma

34. As an employee at a local bank, you accidently learn that a former classmate, Dan, was denied a loan because he was a poor credit risk. You visit your uncle a few days later and learn that he is considering lending Dan $2,000. Your uncle knows Dan's father and believes Dan is a person of good character who would honor a commitment and repay his debts. Would you tell your uncle what you know? Why or why not?

_____

_____

_____

GLOSSARY

A

Annual percentage rate (APR) the *percentage* cost of credit stated on a yearly basis (p. 166)

B

Balance of trade the difference between a country's exports and imports (p. 93)

Balance sheet a financial statement that lists a business's assets (what a company owns) and liabilities (what a company owes) (p. 83)

Benefits compensation in forms other than a direct payment to the employee (p. 76)

Board of directors officers of a corporation, elected by shareholders, who have the responsibility for directing the business of the corporation (p. 42)

Brand name name given to a product or service to distinguish it from other similar products or services (p. 127)

Bribe a forced payment of money or a favor required before an official or decision maker will make a favorable decision (p. 107)

Business budget a detailed plan for meeting the financial needs of the business (p. 80)

Business cycle movement of the economy from one condition to another and back again, including the four phases of prosperity, recession, depression, and recovery (p. 20)

Business ethics rules about how businesses and their employees are expected to behave (pp. 105–106)

Business plan a written description of the business idea and how it will be carried out including all major activities (p. 64)

C

Capitalism economic system in which economic resources are privately owned by individuals rather than by the government (p. 6)

Channel of distribution the path that a product travels as it goes from producer to consumer (p. 49)

Code of ethics a set of rules for guiding the actions of employees or members of an organization (p. 106)

Commercial bank deposit-type financial institution that offers a wide range of financial services (p. 145)

Comparison shopping comparing unit prices, quality, and services associated with one product with those of another (p. 124)

Compensation the amount of money paid to an employee for work performed (p. 75)

Competition rivalry among businesses to sell their products and services to consumers (p. 8)

Consumer a person or business that buys or uses goods and services (p. 118)

Consumer movement the uniting of consumers to get fair treatment from businesses (p. 132)

Contract an agreement to exchange goods and services for something of value, usually money (p. 99)

Corporation business owned by a number of people and operated under written permission from the state that charters it (p. 42)

Credit the privilege of using someone else's money for a period of time (p. 158)

Creditor the one who sells on credit or who grants a loan (p. 158)

D

Debtor anyone who buys on credit or receives a loan (p. 158)

Demand the relationship between the amount of a good or service that consumers are willing and able to buy and the price of the good or service (p. 24)

E

Economic resources the means through which goods and services are produced (p. 11)

Electronic funds transfer (EFT) a system through which funds are moved electronically from one account to another (p. 154)

Embargo a device governments use to regulate international trade that completely stops the export or import of a product or service (p. 96)

Exports goods and services that U.S. companies sell to other countries (p. 93)

Extractor business that takes resources from nature to make its products or for direct consumption (p. 35)

F

Federal Deposit Insurance Corporation (FDIC) federal agency that regulates banks and other financial institutions (pp. 144–145)

Federal Reserve System government agency that supervises and regulates member banks and helps them serve the public efficiently (p. 148)

Finance charge the total *dollar* cost of credit (p. 166)

Financial record a record of the financial performance of a business (p. 82)

Franchise a written contract granting permission to a businessperson to sell someone else's product or service (p. 42)

Fraud occurs when consumers are given false information deliberately in an effort to make a sale (p. 132)

G

Goods things you can see and touch that satisfy needs and wants (p. 11)

Grade a rating given to food that indicates the quality or size of the product (p. 120)

Gross domestic product (GDP) the total dollar value of all goods and services produced in an economy in one year (p. 18)

H

Human relations activities that involve interacting with people (p. 69)

Human resources management business function that involves all aspects of recruiting, hiring, training, compensating, and evaluating employees (p. 72)

I

Imports goods and services that U.S. companies buy from other countries (p. 93)

Impulse buying buying without giving much thought to the purchase (p. 129)

Income statement a financial statement that shows revenues, expenses, and net income (profit) or loss for a certain period of time (p. 82)

Intellectual property property that is purely intangible, with no physical characteristics (p. 100)

Interest the amount charged for borrowing money or the amount the bank pays for use of a depositor's money (p. 155)

Intermediary business involved in selling the goods and services of producers to consumers and other businesses (p. 35)

International business all of the business activities necessary for creating, shipping, and selling goods and services across national borders (p. 92)

L

Label a tag attached to or printed on a product that contains useful information about it (p. 122)

Leadership the ability to influence individuals, groups, or teams to accomplish important goals (p. 67)

M

Manufacturer business that gets supplies from other producers and converts them into its own products (p. 35)

Market economy economic system in which businesses and individuals are free to make their own decisions as they buy and sell in the marketplace (p. 5)

Marketing orientation the concept that businesses consider the needs of customers when developing products and services (p. 48)

Marketing strategy the plan that a company develops to show how it will use marketing to achieve its goals (p. 48)

Markup the amount that is added to the cost of producing a product or service (p. 52)

Money order a form of payment that orders the issuing agency to pay the amount printed on the form to a specified payee (p. 153)

Monopoly environment in which a business has no competition and controls the market for a good or service (p. 133)

N

Needs things required in order to live (p. 10)

P

Partnership business owned and managed by a small group—often not more than two or three people—who have entered into an agreement (p. 41)

Profit the amount of money left over when subtracting the expenses of operating a business from its income (pp. 7–8)

Q

Quota a device governments use to regulate international trade that sets a limit on the quantity of a product that can be imported or exported (p. 95)

S

Scarcity the conflict between unlimited wants and limited resources (p. 4)

Service business business that performs activities that are consumed by customers (p. 35)

Services activities that are consumed at the same time they are produced (p. 11)

Small business an independent business with fewer than 500 employees (p. 60)

Small Business Administration (SBA) government agency that provides services and helpful publications to small businesses (p. 62)

Social responsibility the duty of a business to contribute to the well-being of a community and society at large (p. 108)

Sole proprietorship business owned and operated by one person (p. 40)

Supply the amount of a good or service that businesses are willing and able to provide based on the price of the good or service (p. 24)

T

Target market a group of individuals or businesses that has similar product needs (p. 48)

Tariff a device governments use to regulate international trade that taxes certain imported products to cause their prices to increase in the country's markets (p. 95)

U

Unit price a price per unit of measure, such as price per ounce, pound, quart, or other unit of measure (p. 125)

W

Wants things that are not necessary for survival, but add comfort and pleasure to our lives (pp. 10–11)

Human resources management
  analyze staff needs, 73
  compensation, benefits, and
      evaluation, 75–77
  defined, 72–73
  employee qualifications, determine,
      73–74
  employees, find new, 74–75
  in Japan, 73

I

Ideas, generate, 36, 62
Implied warranty, 134
Imports
  embargoes and, 96
  GDP and, 18
  quotas and, 95
  tariffs and, 95–96
  trade and, 93
Impulse buying, 129
Income, 80
Income statement, 82–83
Income taxes, 102
Indirect channel of distribution, 50
Industrial Revolution, 11
Inflation, 19–20
Informal communication, 70
Information, consumer, where to find,
      118–122
Information management, as marketing
      function, 51
Informed
  consumer responsibility to be, 136
  consumer right to be, 132
Installment interest, 165
Installments, 159
Insurance, as job benefit, 77
Insurance companies, as source of
      consumer information, 121
Intangible property, 100
Intellectual property rights, protecting,
      100
Interest
  defined, 154
  simple, 165
Interest rate, of loan, 164
Interest rates, Federal Reserve and, 149
Intermediaries, 35
Internal communication, 70
Internal Revenue Service, 43–44
International business, 92
  relationships, 110
International currency, 93–94
International trade, barriers to
  embargoes, 96
  quotas, 95
  tariffs, 95–96
Internet
  comparison shopping on, 129
  e-commerce and, 37

online shopping, 121
shopping on, 128
as source of consumer information,
      120
as source of job information, 78
Inventory records, 82
Investment companies, as nondeposit
      institutions, 147
Investments, 156

J

Japan, human resources in, 73
Job applicants, common sources of,
      74–75
Job description, 74
Job evaluation, 77
Job safety, 109
Job satisfaction, importance of
      developing, 70
Joint venture, 43

K

Kennedy, John F. (President), 132
Kiplinger's Personal Finance magazine, 119

L

Label, 122
Labor, unfair practices, 110
Labor productivity, as economic measure,
      18–19
Language translators, 96
Laws
  intellectual property and, 100
  to protect citizen rights, 98
  to protect consumers, 134
  regulating credit, 167–170
Lead a business, 45
Leadership, in the workplace
  characteristics of good leaders, 68
  defined, 67–68
Legal tender, 157
Legality, in contracts, 99
Lemon laws, 134
Lending services, of financial institutions,
      154
Levi Strauss & Co., 32
Liability, 41
Life insurance companies, 146–147
Limited liability, 42, 44
Limited liability company (LLC), 44
Loan credit, 159

M

Mail-in rebates, 121
Mail order shopping, 128
Make Academic Connections
  accounting, 85, 89
  advertising, 31, 53, 130, 141, 150,
      171

art, 175
business law, 104, 115, 137, 141, 157
business literature, 123
business math, 22, 39, 53, 57, 71, 85,
      97, 115, 130, 141, 163, 171
business services, 141
careers, 78, 115
communication, 9, 31, 46, 66, 71, 78,
      89, 163, 171, 175
consumer economics, 57, 85, 150
consumerism, 123
creative writing and art, 57
ecology, 16, 115, 141
economics, 57, 175
English composition, 137
environment, 31
finance, 104
geography, 9
government, 31, 66, 78, 89
international marketing, 111
languages, 97
marketing, 16, 157
problem solving, 31, 46
psychology, 66
research, 9, 22, 27, 39, 141, 157
social studies, 89
sociology, 27
technology, 46, 57, 104, 141
Malaysia, credit cards in, 161
Management, of finances, 79–81
  budgets, 80–81
  financial records, 82–84
Management, of human resources, 72–75
Manufacturers, 35
Market economy
  characteristics of
      competition, 8
      private enterprise, 6
      private property, 7
      profit, 7–8
  defined, 5–6
  United States as, 24
Marketing
  defined, 47
  functions of
      distribution, 50
      financial analysis, 51
      information management, 51
      pricing, 51–52
      product/service management, 50
      promotion, 52
      selling, 50–51
  strategy
      channels, 49
      marketing mix, 48
      orientation, 49
      target market, 48
Marketing assistant career, 32
Marketing channels, 49
Marketing mix, 48